TO

———————————————————————

FROM

———————————————————————

DATE

———————————————————————

WORDS
THAT SHAPED
OUR WORLD

BOOKS AND MOVIES BY JIM STOVALL

The Ultimate Gift
The Ultimate Life
The Ultimate Journey
The Ultimate Legacy
The Millionaire Map
The Ultimate Financial Plan
Ultimate Hindsight
The Gift of a Legacy
A Christmas Snow
Success Secrets of Super Achievers
Today's the Day!
The Art of Learning and Self-Development
The Art of Productivity
The Art of Presentation
The Art of Communication
The Financial Crossroads
Ultimate Productivity
Keeper of the Flame
The Lamp
Poems, Quotes, and Things to Think About
Wisdom of the Ages
Discovering Joye
Top of the Hill
One Season of Hope
Wisdom for Winners Volume 1, 2, 3, 4
100 Worst Employees
The Will to Win
The Art of Entrepreneurship
Passport to Success (with Dr. Greg Reid)
Words That Shaped Our World (with Kathy Johnson)

WORDS THAT SHAPED OUR WORLD

QUOTES THAT CHANGED HOW WE THINK, WHAT WE DO, AND WHO WE ARE

VOLUME 1

JIM STOVALL &
KATHY JOHNSON

Published and distributed by:
SOUND WISDOM
P.O. Box 310
Shippensburg, PA 17257-0310
717-530-2122
info@soundwisdom.com
www.soundwisdom.com

ISBN 13 TP: 978-1-64095-415-1
ISBN 13 eBook: 978-1-64095-416-8

For Worldwide Distribution, Printed in the U.S.A.

1 2 3 4 5 6 7 8 / 26 25 24 23 22

DEDICATION

The authors dedicate this book to the publishers, editors, booksellers, and librarians who create, perfect, and present the written word. These people record our history, preserve our thoughts, and make our world a bigger and better place.

CONTENTS

INTRODUCTION

Jim Stovall and Kathy Johnson

WORDS ARE THE ONLY TOOLS we have to convey our thoughts, ideas, and beliefs. Properly presented, words can be informative, inspiring, and soul stirring, but at best, they are lacking. Words are imperfect, incomplete, and inadequate. Even if everyone on planet Earth spoke the same language, we do not mean the same things when we use specific words. I may communicate that I love my spouse, I love my children, I love my dog, I love my favorite baseball team, or I love pepperoni pizza. Obviously, the depth and breadth of the word *love* can mean a myriad of things when it is written or spoken.

I'm sure you can remember a time when a family member, teacher, or coach gave us a word of encouragement or a quote that made a difference in the moment that remains with us years later. Just as words can inspire and affect you and me as individuals, words can galvanize a country, society, or humanity as a whole. In much the same way a loved one, colleague, or friend can whisper a powerful phrase that connects in our consciousness, there are certain individuals who, throughout history, have found themselves in the time and place to step into the spotlight of the world stage and utter or write words that transcend that time and place and become a powerful part of the collective human experience.

This book is a collection of those words, thoughts, and phrases. The quotes are significant not only for what was said, but for who said it and under what circumstances. I reject the notion of any book, including this one, purporting to be "The Complete Guide to…." This book is not intended to give you anything approaching a complete review of all the words that have altered our world.

Instead, this book is a mere example of the written and spoken offerings that can guide you as you continue to seek and collect wisdom in the form of powerful quotes that have a significant historic context. Within these pages, you and I are going to take a journey together throughout time and space. This journey will explore thoughts, ideas, and concepts boiled down to a few memorable and powerful words that endure.

I am very proud to be joined on this journey by my friend and coauthor Kathy Johnson who is a talented writer, editor, and thought leader in her own right. Kathy is a voracious researcher and a meticulous editor. For more than twenty years, I have written a weekly syndicated column read in newspapers, magazines, and online publications around the world. Each week I am pleased to have Kathy review my thoughts and edit my words before I share them with countless readers globally. As you read each of the entries in this book, please consider not only what the writer or speaker was saying to his or her contemporaries in the moment, but what they are saying to you and me here and now.

—Jim Stovall, 2021

INTRODUCTION

THROUGHOUT TIME, the famous and the not so well known have left us with words that live in our hearts and minds for generations. Like the comedic quotes of Groucho Marx, "Outside of a dog, a book is man's best friend. Inside of a dog it's too dark to read," and, "Quote me as saying I was misquoted," or Mae West's insightful comment, "Too much of a good thing could be wonderful," we repeat their words in casual conversations for a good chuckle.

Some quotes, such as Abraham Lincoln's, "My great concern is not whether you have failed, but whether you are content with your failure," make us reflect on our own accomplishments. Still others, like as the words of Anne Frank, "How wonderful it is that nobody need wait a single moment before starting to improve the world," a world that was taken from her too soon, make us sad remembering the past.

Perhaps the most repeated quotes are the ones that we live by, that shape our lives, and that inspire us to live a more meaningful life, like the words of John Wooden, "Do not let making a living prevent you from making a life."

While historical references live on, so do lines written for television and movies. We find ourselves repeating dialogue in our everyday life.

In Margaret Mitchell's 1936 novel made into one of the greatest American cinematic motion pictures, principal male character, Rhett Butler says to Scarlett O'Hara, "Frankly my dear, I don't give a damn." This line has been repeated countless times.

As you read this book, let the words of those who came before inspire and enlighten you.

—Kathy Johnson, 2021

1

*"The wisdom of the wise, and the experience of ages,
may be preserved by quotations."*

—ISAAC D'ISRAELI, BRITISH AUTHOR

A MAN OF MANY WORDS, Isaac D'Israeli, born in 1766, was a British writer and scholar known for his essays, poems, and associations with other "men of letters"—men of great learning and engaged in literary pursuits, particularly as professional writers.

For more than two centuries, his family thrived as merchants. Through gratitude to the God of Jacob, believed to have shown their ancestors through hardship, they dropped their Gothic surname and adopted the name D'Israeli. The name was chosen to honor their heritage and ensure that it was recognized forever in history. It was a name never been known before or since by any other family. Later in his life, for reasons unknown, Isaac D'Israeli's eldest son, Benjamin, dropped the apostrophe and simplified his name to Disraeli.

Beginning his literary career at age sixteen, Isaac D'Israeli created English adaptations of traditional tales from the Middle East, historical biographies, and numerous poems. His most notable work was his collection of essays entitled, *Curiosities of Literature*, popular in the 19th century. It delighted young readers' enthusiasm for knowledge on many topics. Not readily found elsewhere, the collection sprung forth the extraordinary treasures of his mind. It offered a unique and varied compilation of anecdotes relating to unusual books, historical events, intriguing people, habits of book collectors, and more. After thirty-three years, D'Israeli completed the eight-volume collection in 1824.

In 1828, his book, *The Life and Reign of Charles I*, awarded him the Doctor of Civil Law Degree from the University of Oxford, England.

Within the pages of Isaac D'Israeli's writings is the quote, "The wisdom of the wise and the experience of the ages are preserved by quotations." At age 36, he married Maria, his wife of forty-five years, producing five children, one of which was Benjamin Disraeli, the Earl of Beaconsfield, who later became British prime minister of the United Kingdom from 1874 to 1880. Since 1986, a paraphrased version of the quote has been misattributed to his son, Benjamin.

In 1841, Isaac D'Israeli became blind. He endured an operation believed to restore his sight, but it was unsuccessful. Even so, he continued to write with the help of his daughter, Sarah.

In the winter of 1848, Isaac D'Israeli died of influenza at the age of 81. Thereafter, his daughter-in-law, Mary Anne Lewis, wife of Benjamin, erected a monument in his honor on their eight-thousand-acre estate, known as Hughenden Manor. It is located in High Wycombe, Buckinghamshire; and since 1987, the National Register of Historic Parks and Gardens has welcomed tourists to view the manor and the monument.

Few people would recognize the name Isaac D'Israeli, but any student of history would instantly understand and appreciate his contribution to the world and his legacy. As the father of British Prime Minister Benjamin Disraeli, he impacted the world by impacting a future world leader. His words remind us that wisdom is born out of experience. Often this experience, which brings us wisdom, initially, is filled with pain and regret. Therefore, we can gain wisdom out of our own suffering or we can learn from the experiences of other people.

The fastest way to the mountaintop in any endeavor of life is to collect and compile the wisdom of people who have been where you want to go. This collective wisdom, as Isaac D'Israeli points out, is stored and retained between quotation marks.

2

"The unexamined life is not worth living."

—SOCRATES

GREEK PHILOSOPHER SOCRATES, an insightful and brilliant intellect, was born in Athens, Greece, to a stonemason and a midwife in 469 BC. He was an independent thinker who spent his life rationally examining every aspect of humanity. He once said he devoted himself only to what he regarded as the most important art or occupation, that of "discussing philosophy."

Socrates enjoyed strolling through the open Agora, engaging in conversation with its patrons and merchants. Some considered him charismatic. Others found him irritating, and they thought him to be pious and a threat to religion, for he believed it was not from the generosity of the gods that one would find happiness, but rather it was from within oneself.

Outside the limits of the marketplace, the youth of Athens gathered, as no persons under the age of 18 were permitted within its boundaries. Socrates, worn in his tattered robe and bare feet, engaged in conversation, particularly with the impressionable minds of the young men who were destined to, one day, become future leaders. There, he provoked questions and probed their minds, always playing the fool and pretending to know nothing. His pretense of ignorance evoked more conversation and emotion as he encouraged his fellow man to break down every problem or issue into smaller components, analyze each separately, and ultimately rejoin the parts together to conclude an unquestionable answer. This concept would later be known as the Socratic Method.

Throughout his life, Socrates did not sell his teachings or philosophies for money but instead, he preferred to sustain himself from the handouts of friends. He believed one could not buy knowledge or wisdom, and reading or listening to lectures was not the answer. Knowledge and wisdom came only from a dialog, and in his words, "The only evil is ignorance."

To Socrates' thinking, rooted in ethics, there were only five virtues—justice, temperance, courage, piety, and wisdom—and they were each linked together. Further, he believed that doing the right thing protected one's soul, but to do wrong irreparably harmed it.

In 399 BC, at the age of 70, the community had enough. They put Socrates on trial. There were two charges before him: impiety, claiming that he denied the gods and introduced new ones of his own; and corruption, alleging that he had corrupted the young. These charges carried the heaviest punishment that could be imposed—death.

While Socrates was permitted to defend himself, he soon realized that the odds were stacked against him, saying, "I can't defend myself. It is like boxing with shadows." He was judged by five hundred random men of varied occupations throughout his trial—from the aristocrat to the fishmonger. Not all of the men could intelligently judge.

By secret ballot, Socrates was found guilty and sentenced to execution. While he could have requested a lesser punishment of either a monetary fine or exile, he chose the ultimate sentence—death by hemlock poisoning, saying, "Now I get to die and you to live; God only knows which is the better journey."

Though Socrates' thoughts and words have lived for twenty-five centuries, he never wrote a book or left behind any writings.

His death sentence was intended to silence him, but his words and philosophies live on in history. The one thing that assured Socrates' legacy was the exact thing he disregarded throughout his life—the written word. He challenges us all to "never be thought-less."

Socrates' philosophy continues to be a focus in many people's lives. It is vital to our happiness to live life intentionally.

———— A ————

Every thought leader, personal development writer, or success speaker—including the authors of this book—owe a debt of gratitude to Socrates. As his wisdom has endured for almost 2,500 years, he remains a constant reminder that wisdom never goes out of date or out of style. Countless world leaders and philosophers have influenced the world throughout the ensuing centuries because they stood on the shoulders of Socrates. His quote, *"The unexamined life is not worth living,"* reminds us that the place to begin any journey or success quest is right where we are at any given moment. Unless or until we accept the full responsibility for our past, we cannot completely understand our present or create our own future.

The ability to understand, assess, and examine who we are and where we are is the beginning of all growth. Examining our lives is not a one-time task. It is a lifelong pursuit for those who want to live out their dreams and make a difference in this world. When we consult a map to determine how best to reach our destination, the first step involves determining exactly where we are and identifying our current location.

3

*"No one can be judged except by the backdrop
of the time and place in which they lived."*

—LOUIS L'AMOUR

LOUIS DEARBORN LAMOORE, later taking back the French spelling of his ancestral surname, L'Amour, was a famous American writer. His works include historical fiction, science fiction, nonfiction, short-story collections, and poetry, still in print today. Most people remember him as one of the world's most popular Westerns genre writers, most notable for his novels and movies. Though recognized as a gifted writer of the Westerns genre, he also wrote the historical fiction novel *The Walking Drum*, the science fiction book *Haunted Mesa*, and the nonfiction book *Frontier*.

Born the youngest of seven children to a French-Canadian veterinarian father and Irish mother in 1908, L'Amour spent his first fifteen years on a farm in Jamestown, North Dakota. As a child, he filled his free time reading at the local Alfred E. Dickey Free Library, which fueled his dream of becoming a storyteller. He particularly enjoyed reading books on wars and politics. In school, this gave Louis an advantage over other students and, not surprisingly, over his teachers' knowledge of history, as well.

In 1923, Dr. LaMoore and his wife, Emily, packed up their belongings and their boys, Louis and his adopted brother, John, and headed south. For the majority of that decade, they skinned cattle, baled hay, worked in mines and sawmills and lumber camps all across the country.

Louis performed an assortment of jobs throughout his life, such as a mine assessment worker, merchant seaman, and professional boxer. His impressive career record as a boxer touted fifty-nine fights, five losses, and thirty-four knockouts. Through these experiences and his travels through England, Japan, China, Borneo, the Dutch East Indies, Arabia, Egypt, and Panama, he cast his characters in his books.

Louis L'Amour used his personal experiences growing up on the farm, travel experiences, true stories of the Wild West told to him as a child, newspaper articles published at the time, personal diaries of the people who lived their lives as cowboys and ranchers surviving Indian opposition, and other hardships to create stories that transform us into another time and place.

In 1930, L'Amour settled in Choctaw, Oklahoma, where he started his family and writing career. He brought his characters' words, actions, and personalities to life through his "frontier stories." He once said that if he wrote of a particular place, it was of firsthand knowledge that he could make the imagery true to life.

In his biographical recording, Louis L'Amour explained, "I had never thought of myself as a Western writer. I'd never planned to write about the West, but suddenly, I had a bestseller on my hands."

His accredited words, "No one can be judged except by the backdrop of the time and place in which they lived," are a testament that knowing another person's perspective is the cornerstone to understanding.

He died following his battle with lung cancer on June 10, 1988, and forever, we will remember Louis L'Amour as one of the great storytellers of all time.

CHAPTER 3

— A —

As the best-selling author of more than fifty books, eight of which have been turned into major motion pictures, and as a blind person, I'm embarrassed to admit to my readers around the world that when I could read with my eyes, as you are doing now, via print or an electronic version of this book, I was not a reader. I don't believe I ever read an entire book cover to cover until I was blind and discovered audiobooks, as I participated in a study of compressed digital audio to determine how fast listeners could consume audio content and still retain its meaning and message.

Today, thanks to this amazing technology, I am able to read a complete book every day. Becoming a voracious reader for a quarter of a century made me want to be a writer. It changed my world.

The first author I was drawn to via those early audiobooks, was Louis L'Amour. He is best known for his historical Western novels; and at the time of his death in 1988, at age 80, he was among the best-selling authors of all times. I have read more than a hundred of his novels and have consumed most of them multiple times. I don't believe there's anyone better at putting a reader in another time and place than Louis L'Amour. His quote reminds us that context is the key to understanding any quote or the wisdom contained in those words.

Louis L'Amour was a member of what we now call The Greatest Generation. These people lived through the Great Depression and World War II. I don't believe they were born as The Greatest Generation, but the time and place in which they lived called them to greatness.

To understand anyone's perspective or wisdom in the form of a great quote requires us to understand where, how, and when they lived.

4

"Man is designed for accomplishment, engineered for success, and endowed with the seeds of greatness."

— ZIG ZIGLAR

BEGINNING HIS CAREER selling heavy-duty, waterless cookware door-to-door, Hilary Hinton "Zig" Ziglar became one of America's most famous, upbeat, and enthusiastic sales trainers and motivational speakers. With his Southern drawl and comedic presentation style, he shared concepts, stories, and anecdotes designed to guide people in the insurance, automobile, cosmetic, and financial industries, as well as entrepreneurs and curiosity-seeking individuals, to live a more successful and intentional existence, both on a personal and professional level, and to be their best, always.

On stage, Zig Ziglar shared his "10 Rules for Success." They included the following: have a dream; think as a champion; be committed; do it right now; be prepared; keep your word; set goals; evaluate where you are; have integrity; and do not quit. These were all rules that made him a success. He said that his favorite saying was, "The most important thing you can do is to understand that anything worth doing is worth doing poorly—until you can learn to do it well."

Throughout his life, he wrote more than thirty books. His first, *See You at the Top*, sold more than 1.5 million copies, and it is still in print today.

CHAPTER 4

In addition to his most notable sales-related books, he also wrote: *Raising Positive Kids in a Negative World; Courtship After Marriage: Romance Can Last a Lifetime;* and being no stranger to grief he wrote, *Confessions of a Grieving Christian.*

Early in his life, Zig Ziglar faced tragedies that could have derailed his zest for life. Even with the loss of his father at age five, his sister's death one year later, and his daughter's death due to an illness, he did not let that happen. He maintained a positive spirit and shared it with others.

In 2007, after a nasty fall down a flight of stairs, Zig Ziglar was left with short-term memory problems, but he continued to take the stage until his retirement in 2010.

Though we no longer have the privilege of hearing Zig Ziglar share his formulas for success performed live on stage, we can continue to listen to his uplifting and motivational speeches through his books, presentation packages, and recordings. His legacy lives on.

———— A ————

I remember as a teenager going to the performing arts center in my hometown and sitting in the front row for a Zig Ziglar event. I had never experienced anything like Zig or his powerful motivational message, so you can imagine how meaningful it was to me years later to be able to share the stage with him when I was speaking at a motivational event.

As an author, speaker, and movie producer, I have had the opportunity to meet many high-profile people. Unfortunately, some of them I wish I had never met, as their private lives do not mirror their public persona. When I got to know Zig Ziglar personally, I discovered he was everything I'd hoped he'd be and more.

I remember sitting backstage at an arena event waiting for my turn to speak. It was one of those days. Everything seemed to be going wrong. The sound wasn't working right, they couldn't get the lighting adjusted, and the stage manager was panicking.

Zig came in the back door of the arena with his standard greeting to everyone, "It's a great day today."

The frazzled stage manager responded in a snide and sarcastic tone, "Well, you're in a good mood today, aren't you?" The backstage area fell silent, and everyone was awaiting Zig's response.

He smiled, turned to the stage manager and said, "Yes, I'm having a great day today because over twenty years ago, I decided to have a great day today."

The stage manager challenged, "I think that motivational speeches are temporary and all of the positive thoughts wear off."

Zig chuckled and responded, "I agree that the results of motivation are temporary just like the results of bathing, which is why we recommend both on a daily basis."

5

"If it is to be, it is up to me."

—WILLIAM H. JOHNSEN

THOUGH NOT MUCH is known about William H. Johnsen, he is recognized as the author of the well-known quote, "If it is to be, it is up to me."

What is written about William H. Johnsen is that he was born in Holstein, Germany, on October 6, 1853, and he served in the German Army while in his twenties. For most of his career, he worked as a carpenter, primarily holding the title of ship's carpenter on various sailing vessels.

It has been noted that Johnsen sailed to England, Cuba, and the United States using his carpentry skills aboard the ships he traveled. He made his way to California in 1877. A year later, after a busy and useful life, he settled with his wife and two daughters on an eighty-acre farm in San Joaquin County, California. An avid believer in education, Johnsen served as a trustee of the Jefferson school district.

Keeping with the spirit of his words, William H. Johnsen led an intentional life in a way that suited him.

—— A ——

"If it is to be, it is up to me," is among the unique phrases in the English language. There may be no other ten-word sentence

made up of entirely two-letter words. These are small words with a huge impact. The beginning of all success and achievement is taking personal responsibility.

Unless and until you and I are willing to accept full responsibility for our past and own the fact that our current situation is a result of all of our decisions and actions up to the present moment, we cannot take advantage of the fact that tomorrow can be anything we want it to be based upon the decisions we make today.

As a blind person, I am keenly aware of the fact that bad things happen to good people. However, for everyone distracted, detoured, or defeated by a personal or professional challenge, I can show you other people who have faced that same challenge and used it as a springboard to greater success.

6

"Every adversity, every failure, every heartbreak carries with it the seed of an equal or greater benefit."

—NAPOLEON HILL

AS THE AUTHOR of the best-selling book, *Think and Grow Rich*, published in 1937, Napoleon Hill shared his thirteen essential principles to improve one's life. His philosophies have cast a long shadow through generations.

He was born Oliver Napoleon Hill on October 26, 1883, in a one-room cabin in southwest Virginia, and he began writing as a "mountain reporter" for his father's newspaper when he was 13 years old. When he graduated from high school, he relocated to Tazewell, Virginia, to attend business school; and in 1901, he landed a job working in a law office. Later, he cofounded the Acree-Hill Lumber Company, moving on to launch the Automobile College of Washington upon moving to Washington, DC.

After a series of losses, it has been reported that the turning point of Hill's life was in 1908 when he interviewed the powerful industrialist and philanthropist Andrew Carnegie. During the interview, the man challenged Napoleon Hill to interview wealthy and successful people of the time to discover a common thread for achieving success. Interviewees included Henry Ford, Alexander Graham Bell, Thomas A. Edison, and scientists Elmer R. Gates and Luther Burbank from whom he sought insight.

What was it that made successful people achieve so much? Napoleon Hill spent the next twenty years honing in on the formula to develop the tools essential to improve one's life. In the process, he discovered the "secret," and he shared its essence in his book. He did not serve up the secret but shared the following:

> If you truly desire money so keenly that your desire is an obsession, you will have no difficulty in convincing yourself that you will acquire it. The object is to want money, and to be so determined to have it that you convince yourself that you will have it. ...You may as well know, right here, that you can never have riches in great quantities unless you work yourself into a white heat of desire for money and actually believe you will possess it.

As a young man, Napoleon Hill married Florence Elizabeth Horner, and they had three sons, James, Napoleon Blair, and David. Blair's condition inspired his Think and Grow Rich Principle 2—Faith. The child was born without ears—absent of external ears and the auditory canal. Napoleon Hill knew that once he identified his specific desire to do whatever it took to ensure his son's hearing would be restored, it was essential to have the faith to fuel that desire.

It was with his strong desire, abundant faith, and his silent vow to see that his son would grow up like other children that he set out to make it happen. Through continuous efforts, spinal manipulation, and ultimately a special hearing device, Blair's hearing was restored. He, then, had grown up able to hear and speak almost normally. Blair went on to encourage and help others like him to hear the fascinating world around them.

CHAPTER 6

On November 8, 1970, Napoleon Hill died at the age of 87 with an estimated net worth of one million dollars. However, through his words and legacy, millions of men and women continue to achieve success, earning well over that of Napoleon Hill.

Napoleon Hill had many losses and disappointments throughout his life, but through the adversities, failures, and heartbreaks, things of equal or greater benefit arose.

Today, there is a foundation named in his honor. The Napoleon Hill Foundation is a nonprofit educational institution designed to help individuals realize their full potential professionally and personally. Through his books and those who have carried on his teachings and philosophies, the foundation encourages people of all ages to take the steps necessary to make their goals a reality.

———— A ————

Napoleon Hill is among the most influential people in my life and the lives of countless people around the world. He was born in the 19th century, wrote his monumental book, *Think and Grow Rich* in the 20th century, and his words and thoughts continue to impact people here in the 21st century. I've been proud to feature Napoleon Hill: in one of my historical novels entitled *Top of the Hill*; write a book entitled *Dear Napoleon*, which explores the impact his work has had on people from every walk of life; and feature in the documentary film, *Think and Grow Rich The Legacy*, which highlights his continuing influence around the world.

As a college student, I was introduced to one of my mentors, Lee Braxton, who despite only having a third-grade education, became a wealthy entrepreneur and philanthropist. Before he would begin mentoring me, Mr. Braxton required that I read Napoleon Hill's book, *Think and Grow Rich*, three times. It became the basis for everything he taught me.

Long after Mr. Braxton's death, I wrote a book titled *The Millionaire Map*, recounting my journey from poverty to prosperity to purpose. Don Green, executive director of the Napoleon Hill Foundation, contacted me and asked, "Did you know your mentor, Lee Braxton, was Napoleon Hill's best friend, and he gave the eulogy at Dr. Hill's funeral?" I was shocked to learn this and told Don I had not been aware of it. Don Green shared with me a file of letters that Napoleon Hill and Mr. Braxton exchanged over more than thirty years. I treasure these letters and feel that they are a connection between me and the life and legacy of Napoleon Hill.

7

HIS BIRTH NAME was Samuel Langhorne Clemens, but who has not heard of the American writer, lively storyteller, humorist, entrepreneur, publisher, and lecturer—the man who became Mark Twain?

Mark Twain had the unique ability to make each character in his stories come to life through humor, embellishment, hyperbole, parody, and fundamental truths of nature captured from people he knew or met throughout his life and in his travels around the world. In the humorous fashion only Mark Twain could deliver, he created one-of-a-kind characters, some lacking education but strong at heart.

Samuel Clemens, the sixth of seven children, was born in 1835 in Florida, Missouri. When he was four, the Clemens family moved to Hannibal, Missouri, a port town on the Mississippi River. It was his inspiration for the fictional town of St. Petersburg, the setting in his books, *The Adventures of Tom Sawyer* and *The Adventures of Huckleberry Finn*.

In Twain's memoir, *Life on the Mississippi*, published in 1883, he recounts his days as a steamboat pilot on the Mississippi River before the American Civil War. In it he writes, "There is but one permanent ambition...to be a steam boatman." He further writes, "Pilot was the grandest position of all. The pilot, even in those days of trivial wages, had a princely salary—from a $150 to $250 a month, and no board to pay," he added.

While piloting a steamboat, Samuel Clemens acquired his pen name, Mark Twain. It was a familiar shout on a steamboat, as the leadsman would cry out for a measured river depth of two fathoms—two being the definition of twain. A twain was the mark of a safe twelve feet of water for a steamboat. Thus, mark twain was conceived.

Throughout his life, Mark Twain used his work experiences and travels as his preferred manner of education. After the fifth grade, he quit school to become a printer's apprentice; and later, he began working as a typesetter. He contributed columns and humorous sketches to the *Hannibal Journal*, a newspaper that his brother and secretary of Nevada Territory, Orion, owned. Moreover, he educated himself in public libraries in his spare time, finding broader information than a conventional school.

In his first book, *The Innocents Abroad*, Mark Twain wrote of the yearlong excursion aboard the first-class, side-wheel steamship, "Quaker City," in 1869. For the price of $1,250 and five dollars per day, in gold, for all traveling expenses onshore, passengers selected for the journey could, "Excursion to The Holy Land, Egypt, The Crimea, Greece, and Intermediate Points of Interest." Not only was Mark Twain able to visit Europe and the East, but his trip was chronicled in the *Daily Alta California* of San Francisco and documented and published in a sixty-one chapter book with 234 illustrations.

Mark Twain is known for his wit and satire, prose and speech. He earned praise from critics, peers, presidents, artists, industrialists, and European royalty. Upon hearing of his death, President William Howard Taft said, "Mark Twain gave pleasure—real intellectual enjoyment—to millions, and his works will continue to give such pleasure to millions yet to come… His humor was American, but Englishmen and people of other countries nearly as much appreciated him as his countrymen. He has made an enduring part of American literature."

CHAPTER 7

For his contributions, Mark Twain was awarded an honorary Doctorate of Letters by the University of Oxford in 1907.

As he reached the twilight of his years, Mark Twain said of his time on Earth, "I came in with Halley's Comet in 1835. It is coming again next year, and I expect to go out with it. It will be the greatest disappointment of my life if I don't go out with Halley's Comet. The Almighty has said, no doubt: 'Now here are these two unaccountable freaks; they came in together, they must go out together.'"

Sadly, Mark Twain's prediction was accurate. He died of a heart attack on April 21, 1910, one day after Halley's Comet's closest approach to Earth.

—— A ——

I'm a huge believer in formal education. For more than thirty years, I've funded a private scholarship that has helped more than 500 young people attend college. I realized one of my lifelong goals when I funded and organized the Stovall Center for Entrepreneurship at my alma mater, Oral Roberts University. We offer young people from around the world undergraduate and graduate degrees in entrepreneurship. One of the things I tell all of the incoming students, when I speak to them, is the fact that "This program will give you an education, which is the basic foundation from which you can begin the process of becoming a lifelong learner."

Education brings us knowledge; life experience brings us wisdom. Knowledge is the process of internalizing information. Wisdom is the process of applying information in the real world. As in many areas of the human experience, Mark Twain used his wit and wisdom to bring us a deep, underlying truth.

8

*"Live in such a way that you would not be ashamed
to sell your parrot to the town gossip."*

—WILL ROGERS

SO MUCH HAS BEEN WRITTEN by and about Will Rogers that readers may come to believe they know him personally. With his smiling eyes and boyish grin, he entertained young and old with his pointed humor and puns, homespun philosophy, Oklahoma twang, and southern dialect, all the while spinning his lasso and yarns chewing on a blade of straw. He was "Oklahoma's Favorite Son," and in his traditional cowboy fashion, he performed for audiences worldwide until his tragic death in 1935.

He was born William Penn Adair Rogers in 1879 to a Cherokee family on the Dog Iron Ranch in northeastern Oklahoma Indian Territory, today known as Oologah. The youngest of eight children, he was named for the Cherokee leader, Colonial William Penn Adair. Will Rogers, the only son of Clem and Mary Rogers, lived with three siblings—sisters—who survived into adulthood in a house known as the "White House of the Verdigris River," built in 1875.

In school, he was a good student and an avid reader of *The New York Times*. He attended Willow Hassel School at Neosho and the Kemper Military School and College in Boonville, Missouri. He dropped out after the tenth grade to work on the Dog Iron Ranch.

At 22, he left home and traveled to Argentina in hopes of working as a gaucho. Along with a friend, they spent five months trying their hands as ranch owners, but they could not make a go of it and lost all of their money. He later said, "I was ashamed to send home for more."

That failure led Will Rogers to sail for South Africa, where he began his show business career as a trick roper. The first gag he ever pulled, according to Rogers, was when he got his rope tangled up during a performance and said in his comic banter style, "A rope ain't bad to get tangled up in if it ain't around your neck."

Landing a job in "Texas Jack's Wild West Circus," it was not long before he was itching to move on, and he found himself in Australia. Taking all that he had learned from Texas Jack, he performed with the "Wirth Brothers Circus." There, he not only performed rope tricks, but he perfected his pony act, spinning rope tricks while riding. His nonchalant acting style made it appear to audiences that being a ropin' cowboy was easy.

Will Rogers was so talented with a rope that he was listed in the *Guinness Book of World Records* for throwing three lassos at once—one went around the horse's neck, another circled the rider, and the third flew under the horse, looping all four of its legs together. What kid would not want to become a wrangler like Will Rogers?

He returned to the United States in 1904, first appearing at the St. Louis World's Fair, and it sparked his career on the vaudeville circuits. As he performed, he would ask, "Well, what shall I talk about? I ain't got anything funny to say. All I know is what I read in the papers."

Will Rogers often poked fun at gangsters, lawyers, prohibition, politicians, prominent people, government programs, and other controversial topics in such a manner that it did not offend people. His jokes and puns, inspired through his observations of current events, brought him notoriety.

Will Rogers joined the cast of Florenz Ziegfeld's Midnight Frolic in 1915; and by 1916, he was its featured star on Broadway. As he transitioned from his rope act to satire, he became known as the "Talkin' Fool," rather than the "Ropin' Fool" to his audiences.

Through his recognition in vaudeville, at 44, he landed roles in motion pictures, both in silent and later talkies, making a total of seventy throughout his career. In 1918, he made his first silent film, *Laughing Bill Hyde*, followed by forty-seven more. When the talkies were introduced in 1929, Will Rogers was, once again, able to showcase his verbal wit and keen perception, resulting in becoming one of the top stars and highest-paid actors of the time.

Will Rogers was an iconic American and a role model for his high moral tone. He symbolized stability, and he truly lived his life in such a way that he would not be ashamed to sell his parrot to the town gossip.

His appeal was so influential with the average American that he was once nominated for governor of Oklahoma but declined. While the political office was not his passion, Will Rogers served as a goodwill ambassador to Mexico, and he had a brief stint as mayor of Beverly Hills.

In 1928, he used his column in *Life*, a weekly humor magazine, to run a mock campaign for the presidency, running as the "bunkless candidate" of the Anti-Bunk Party. His only campaign promise was that if he were elected, he would resign. From Memorial Day through Election Day, he "caricatured the farcical humor of grave campaign politics" in his weekly articles. On Election Day, he declared himself victorious and kept his promise. Although he did not receive any state electoral votes, he resigned. His individualism and humor made him admired as the "common man."

In early August 1935, Will Rogers asked his friend and pioneer aviator, Wiley Post, to fly him through Alaska searching for new material for his newspaper column. In his experimental hybrid Lockheed Orion-Explorer seaplane, Post soared through the skies while Rogers wrote his columns on his typewriter.

On August 15, approximately twenty miles southwest of what was then called Point Barrow, Alaska, both Will Rogers and Wiley Post lost their lives in a plane crash. Due to bad weather, they had decided to land in a lagoon to ask for directions. On takeoff, at low altitude, the aircraft plunged, shearing off the right wing and inverting them into the shallow water. Both men died instantly. Our stage and film actor, vaudeville performer, humorist, newspaper columnist, social commentator, and beloved cowboy had left behind his wife, Betty, and two living children, Will Jr., who portrayed his father in *The Story of Will Rogers* in 1952, and Jimmy.

Will Rogers once said, "When I die, my epitaph, or whatever you call those signs on gravestones, is going to read: 'I joked about every prominent man of my time, but I never met a man I didn't like.' I am so proud that I can hardly wait to die so it can be carved."

Numerous sculptures, statues, and monuments, including the "Will Rogers Shrine of the Sun," an 80-foot observation tower high atop the Cheyenne Mountain west of Colorado Springs, at the base of Pikes Peak, have been erected in his honor. Thirteen high schools in Oklahoma and the Will Rogers Turnpike, a section of Interstate 44 between Tulsa, Oklahoma, and Joplin, Missouri, were named for him.

In addition, two airports bear his namesake—the Will Rogers World Airport in Oklahoma City, and in honor of him and his friend, the Wiley Post-Will Rogers Memorial Airport in Alaska, not far from the crash site.

On November 4, 1948, the United States Post Office commemorated Will Rogers with a three-cent postage stamp; and in 1979, it issued a fifteen-cent stamp of him as part of the Performing Arts series.

To this day, fans can visit both his childhood home and his family tomb at the Will Rogers Memorial Museum and Birthplace Ranch in Claremore, Oklahoma.

————— A —————

I was born and raised in Tulsa, Oklahoma, where I make my home today. Arguably, the most famous Oklahoman of all time was Will Rogers. There is no one alive today who is as popular or widely admired as Will Rogers was during his lifetime. He was an author, broadcaster, movie star, columnist, and the most respected voice of reason regarding political matters and issues of the day.

I have written a number of novels in my Homecoming Historical series. Each of these stories takes place at a modern-day high school, and the namesake of the school gets involved with the students in fun and unique ways. Among my favorite of these novels is *Will to Win*, which features Will Rogers and dozens of his poignant and timeless quotes.

Will Rogers' words remind us that we can never overshadow our own reputations. We did exhaustive research in writing the *Will to Win* novel, and in working with the scholars at the Will Rogers Memorial Museum—as well as other sources around the world—we could not find one hint of scandal or controversy surrounding Will Rogers. This is unique and refreshing in the world of celebrities, world leaders, and icons.

9

"This was their finest hour."

—WINSTON CHURCHILL

"THIS WAS THEIR FINEST HOUR," was the name of the speech Winston Churchill, prime minister of the United Kingdom from 1940 to 1945, delivered in Parliament to the House of Commons on June 18, 1940, approximately one month after taking office. In his third speech presented as prime minister, he addressed the success of the "Battle of France." He justified the low level of support the United Kingdom had provided France during the World War II battle. He expressed the successful evacuation of the British Army and 120,000 supporting French military forces with only the loss of equipment. He reminded them that "they have suffered severely, but fought well." He also expressed that Great Britain must move past it and that, "We have to think of the future, and not of the past." It was in his summary that Winston Churchill presented these words:

> Let us, therefore, brace ourselves to our duties, and
> so bear ourselves that if the British Empire and its
> Commonwealth last for a thousand years, men will still
> say, "This was their finest hour."

Winston Churchill, born at Blenheim Palace in Oxfordshire, England, on November 30, 1874, has been recognized as the most extraordinary prime minister of the nineteenth century. When he took office at the age of 77, he was not in good health, as he had suffered several minor strokes. Nonetheless, he was considered a military genius for his extraordinary persistence and tenacity—despite his quirks, sporadic childishness, and reputation for his persistent pleasurable indulgences of cigar smoking and wetting his whistle, for which he made no apologies.

It is reported that, on a month-long visit to 1600 Pennsylvania Avenue hosted by President and Mrs. Franklin Roosevelt, Winston Churchill instructed the butler, "I must have a tumbler of sherry in my room before breakfast, a couple of glasses of scotch and soda before lunch, and French champagne and 90-year-old brandy before I go to sleep at night." Later, the first lady wrote, "It was astonishing to me that anyone could smoke so much and drink so much and keep perfectly well."

The people of Great Britain had great respect for Winston Churchill. Queen Elizabeth, upon the news that Winston Churchill retired in 1955—a mere two years after she had knighted him "Sir" Winston Leonard Spencer Churchill, the British leader who guided Great Britain and the Allies through the crisis of World War II—sent a heartfelt handwritten letter telling him how much she would miss him.

In addition to having high military intellect and razor-sharp wit, Winston Churchill was a brilliant orator, masterful politician, and an accomplished amateur artist known under the pseudonym Charles Morin. He was an avid historian and a prize-winning writer. In 1953, he received the Nobel Prize in Literature for his "mastery of historical and biographical description."

Under Winston S. Churchill or Winston Spencer Churchill, he published a novel, two biographies, three volumes of memoirs, several historical writings, and numerous press articles. His most famous works, which brought him international fame, were his twelve-volume memoir, *The Second World War*, and the four-volume, *A History of the English-Speaking Peoples*.

There was a tamer side to Winston Churchill. He had many hobbies, including his enthusiasm as an amateur bricklayer, for which he erected buildings and garden walls at his Chartwell country home, and his love for butterflies that he seasonally bred in a converted summerhouse each year. He also had several pets, including cats, dogs, pigs, lambs, chickens, goats, and fox cubs.

On January 12, 1965, Winston Churchill endured his final stroke. He died twelve days later, on January 24. He was given a state funeral six days later, going down in history as the first non-royal person to receive such an honor since 1935. Since his death, countless memorials have been dedicated in his honor worldwide.

Winston Churchill was one of only eight people granted honorary citizenship in the United States. He is remembered as the person who rallied the British people and led the country from the brink of defeat to a certain victory.

———— A ————

Winston Churchill may well be the most widely quoted historical figure of all time. Those of us who enjoy freedom, democracy, and capitalism owe a great debt of gratitude to Winston Churchill. I was inspired to write the book you are reading right now when I read a book entitled, *The Power of Words*, which featured direct written and spoken quotes from Winston Churchill throughout more than sixty years of his public life. At one of the darkest times during the depths of World War II, Churchill called on allied soldiers and citizens to seize the moment and make it their finest hour.

Some people realize that there are critical moments in life. Fewer people recognize that we can take advantage of these critical moments, but there are a rare group of powerful individuals like Winston Churchill who understood that we can not only seize the moment, but we can create our finest hour whenever we dedicate ourselves to expending our best efforts in a worthy cause.

10

*"Ask not what your country can do for you,
but what you can do for your country."*

—JOHN F. KENNEDY

MOST EVERYONE KNOWS where they were when they heard the news that our president, John "Jack" Fitzgerald Kennedy, often referred to by his initials JFK, had been shot on November 22, 1963. The former senator from Massachusetts became our 35th president of the United States from 1961 until his death. He was an iconic figure from the long-past time when Americans hung photographs of our leaders on the walls of their family homes. More recent generations only have pictures or the memory of being told of his horrific assassination while riding in the presidential motorcade through Dealey Plaza in Dallas, Texas.

Before becoming president, JFK had a successful military career in the United States Navy, among other courses of action and career achievements throughout his life, such as journalist, author, and politician. It was through his bravery and heroic conduct that the then, Lieutenant Junior Grade officer was awarded the Navy and Marine Corps Medal and the prestigious Purple Heart for the injuries he sustained when a Japanese destroyer in World War II rammed his Patrol Torpedo boat (PT-109). It was through his courage, endurance, and leadership actions that his surviving ten-man crew was saved when he swam many hours, sometimes towing a crewmember by his lifejacket strap clenched between his teeth, to secure aid and food before being rescued.

Some may also recall that JFK was an accomplished author before his presidency. He won the Pulitzer Prize for history in 1957 with his book, *Profiles in Courage*. Later, after witnessing firsthand Great Britain's failed policy of appeasement, JFK transformed his experiences into his graduate thesis. Upon retooling his written dissertation in the 1940s, *Why England Slept* became a bestseller. In all, JFK penned more than thirty books and writings throughout his life.

Elected president of the United States on January 20, 1961, John Fitzgerald Kennedy stood before the crowd gathered at the Capitol. Camera crews televised the first-ever inauguration, and he recited the oath of office. In the speech that followed, his words will be remembered throughout history. In it, he said:

> In the long history of the world, only a few generations have been granted the role of defending freedom in its hour of maximum danger. I do not shrink from this responsibility—I welcome it. I do not believe that any of us would exchange places with any other people or any other generation. The energy, the faith, the devotion, which we bring to this endeavor, will light our country and all who serve it—and the glow from that fire can truly light the world.
>
> And so, my fellow Americans: ask not what your country can do for you—ask what you can do for your country.

The newly elected president went on to address all citizens of the world with the same challenge, "My fellow citizens of the world: ask not what America will do for you, but what together we can do for the freedom of man."

CHAPTER 10

John Fitzgerald Kennedy should be remembered for what he accomplished in his lifetime—albeit brief—not by his sudden and tragic death.

— A —

One of my earliest memories is being a 5-year-old when I learned that President Kennedy had been assassinated. I had little understanding of the gravity of the situation, but I do remember the iconic photo of 3-year-old John Kennedy Jr. saluting this father's flag-draped casket. Many years later, when I was on a book tour for one of my literary projects, I was waiting to be on a talk show in New York and met JFK Jr. In the green room, we were both waiting to be interviewed. I brought up my memory of him in that famous photo. He shared with me that as a 3-year-old at the time, he had no understanding of what had happened, but his father had always trained him to salute the American flag, which is what he did on that fateful day.

JFK's quote, *"Ask not what your country can do for you, but what you can do for your country,"* reminds us that it is better to give than to receive, and this is certainly true when we consider serving our country.

11

"So, first of all, let me assert my firm belief that the only thing we have to fear is...fear itself."

—FRANKLIN DELANO ROOSEVELT

FRANKLIN DELANO ROOSEVELT, the 32nd president of the United States, gave his first inauguration speech on March 4, 1933, symbolizing his first presidential term in office. It marked the last inauguration held on the constitutionally prescribed date before Inauguration Day was forever moved to January 20.

For Americans, it was a time in history when banks had failed, and people were unemployed—it was the Great Depression. In his speech, Franklin Roosevelt outlined his plan to end the suffering in America with a series of programs, financial reforms, regulations, and public works projects that he referred to as the *New Deal*. His twenty-minute speech assured people that there was nothing to fear, and it began like this:

> I am certain that my fellow Americans expect that on my induction into the Presidency, I will address them with a candor and a decision which the present situation of our Nation impels. This is preeminently the time to speak the truth, the whole truth, frankly and boldly. Nor need we shrink from honesty facing conditions in our country today. This great Nation

will endure as it has endured, will revive, and will prosper. *So, first of all, let me assert my firm belief that the only thing we have to fear is...fear itself*—nameless, unreasoning, unjustified terror which paralyzes needed efforts to convert retreat into advance. In every dark hour of our national life, a leadership of frankness and of vigor has met with that understanding and support of the people themselves, which is essential to victory. And I am convinced that you will again give that support to leadership in these critical days.

These words came when the American people needed a leader to ease their uneasiness of the times. Franklin Roosevelt's goal was to turn fear into confidence.

In 1921, years before his presidency, the Roosevelts were vacationing at Campobello Island when he fell ill. His diagnosis—poliomyelitis, although it is believed that he was misdiagnosed and suffered from the autoimmune neuropathy disease known as Guillain-Barré syndrome. As a result, the disease left him paralyzed and wheelchair-bound for the rest of his life. Impressed by the betterment of his condition through hydrotherapy treatments, Franklin Roosevelt established a rehabilitation center at Warm Springs, Georgia.

In 1938, Franklin Roosevelt founded the National Foundation for Infantile Paralysis to combat polio for Americans. Today, his nonprofit organization is known as the March of Dimes. Through Jonas Salk's vaccination, funded by the organization, the United States has been polio-free since 1979. The March of Dimes has expanded over time to focus on research and the prevention of birth defects, infant mortality, and preterm births so that no family will live in fear of losing precious children. Franklin Roosevelt's legacy lives on.

——— A ———

Franklin Delano Roosevelt was elected four times. People of my parents' generation grew up knowing no other president than FDR. He was a towering figure who held our country together during the depths of the Great Depression and the struggles of World War II. His powerful speeches and emotional "fireside chat" radio broadcasts both calmed and encouraged Americans at a critical point in time.

FDR's powerful words about fear remind us now, as they did then, that we can control our emotions and deny fear the opportunity to ruin our lives and disrupt our future. During the Great Depression and World War II, there were certainly challenges that had to be faced, but facing challenges with focus and faith is always better than allowing fear to rule the day.

12

"To be, or not to be: that is the question."

—WILLIAM SHAKESPEARE

WILLIAM SHAKESPEARE was an English poet, actor, and playwright in the Elizabethan Jacobean era, the latter part of the 16th century and early 17th century. Born in Stratford-upon-Avon in the West Midlands region of the United Kingdom, his actual birth date is unknown. However, traditionally, it is observed on April 23—Saint George's Day—a day celebrated in England and twenty-three countries worldwide with a feast in honor of its patron saint. Based on the historical recount, he died, coincidentally, on the same date in 1616.

Though he was not fully celebrated in his time, he is considered the most excellent writer of the English language, producing approximately thirty-nine plays, 154 sonnets, three long-narrative poems. He has been dubbed the "Bard of Avon." His plays have been translated into every major language, and his stories are produced again, and again, through stage productions and movies today. William Shakespeare spanned the scope of genres with comedies, histories, and romances. Some of the best-known plays he produced were tragedies, such as *Hamlet*, *Romeo and Juliet*, *Othello*, *King Lear*, and *Macbeth*.

In his longest play, *The Tragedy of Hamlet, Prince of Denmark (commonly known as Hamlet)*, we hear William Shakespeare's most famous quote, "To be, or not to be: that is the question."

In Act III, Scene 1, Prince Hamlet ponders death over life after having his heart broken—to live or to die. He weighs whether it is better to suffer the slings and arrows of life or to forever sleep and end the heartaches of the flesh by death or suicide. This is a dilemma all too commonly faced by many throughout time.

Two days following his death, William Shakespeare was buried in the chancel of the Holy Trinity Church. In his poet fashion, upon the stone slab that covers his grave, he had these words inscribed:

Good friend, for Jesus' sake forbear,

To dig the dust enclosed here.

Blessed be the man that spares these stones,

And cursed be he that moves my bones.

He died at the age of 52. No cause of death was determined. It has been reported that in his will written one month prior, he began by stating that he was in "perfect health." It has also been said that one of the tributes from fellow authors of the time expressed his sad and sudden demise this way: "We wondered, Shakespeare, that thou went'st so soon—from the world's stage to the grave's tiring room."

William Shakespeare left behind a legacy that lives on in modern theatre. He is remembered by his own words.

Every novelist, moviemaker, and storyteller—including me—owes a great debt of gratitude to William Shakespeare. Arguably, no one has ever reached the height of emotion or depth of character development that Shakespeare achieved in his work. You may not be fully aware of or totally appreciate Shakespeare's stories, but if you haven't experienced them directly, you have enjoyed them written through the lens of other authors with different settings and other character names. His stories will endure as long as human beings share experiences, relationships, and emotions with one another.

In his simple question, *"To be or not to be,"* Shakespeare deals with the most fundamental struggle between life and death. I have long believed that when you are facing a difficult choice between two options, it is far better to select the option that gives you flexibility and the possibility of more choices in the future. Using this logic it is always better to be than not to be.

My academic training is in the field of psychology, and I understand many of the factors that surround the suicide epidemic we are facing in our society. However, whatever circumstance a person may be dealing with, it is important to realize that other people who have faced the same conditions have not only survived, but have thrived in the future. Where there is life there is always hope.

13

"I have learned over the years that when one's mind is made up, this diminishes fear."

—ROSA PARKS

ROSA LOUISE MCCAULEY PARKS was an African-American activist at a time of racial unrest in the United States. Born February 4, 1913, in Tuskegee, Alabama, she was raised on a farm in Montgomery, along with her younger brother, Sylvester, by her maternal grandparents and mother. She grew up to be an American icon in the Civil Rights Movement of the 1950s.

In 1955, a seamstress employed in a department store and wife to Raymond Parks, Rosa Parks was politically savvy. She had been elected secretary of the Montgomery Chapter of the National Association for the Advancement of Colored People (NAACP) and was well respected. Dignified and quiet by nature, Rosa Parks will always be remembered as the black woman who refused to give up her seat on the bus for a white passenger.

On December 1, 1955, Rosa Parks was arrested and charged with disorderly conduct for civil disobedience, when the bus driver ordered her to vacate her seat in the colored section of the city bus, along with three other passengers in the same row, to allow an onboarding white passenger to sit. She violated Chapter 6, Section 11 Segregation Law of the Montgomery City Code. The other three complied, but Rosa Parks refused.

In her autobiography, *My Story,* she explained:

> People always say that I didn't give up my seat because
> I was tired, but that isn't true. I was not tired physically
> or no more tired than I usually was at the end of a
> working day. I was not old, although some people have
> an image of me as being old then. I was forty-two. No,
> the only tired I was, was tired of giving in.

A trial was held the next day. It lasted only thirty minutes, and afterward, she was found guilty and fined $10, in addition to $4 in court costs. In today's currency, that amount would be estimated at approximately $135. Rosa Parks appealed her conviction and formally challenged the legality of racial segregation. In an interview with *National Public Radio* in 1992, she recalled the incident, saying:

> I did not want to be mistreated. I did not want to
> be deprived of a seat that I had paid for. It was just
> time...there was an opportunity for me to take a stand
> to express the way I felt about being treated in that
> manner. I had not planned to get arrested. I had plenty
> to do without having to end up in jail. But when I had
> to face the decision, I didn't hesitate to do so because
> I felt that we had endured that too long. The more
> we gave in, the more we complied with that kind of
> treatment, the more oppressive it became.

Rosa Parks was not the first to refuse to give up her seat on a Montgomery city bus. Months earlier, at least eight others were arrested and charged with the same violation. However, the support Rosa Parks received from her peers prompted her national recognition. Though she did not instigate the protest, the incident incited the Montgomery Bus Boycott on December 5, 1955—a boycott that lasted for thirteen months.

The Montgomery Improvement Association (MIA) was newly formed, and its members elected Martin Luther King Jr., as their president. The organization distributed leaflets the day after the trial asking all black commuters to "Please stay off the buses." On that rainy day, forty-thousand men, women, and children arranged alternative transportation, including taking cabs operated by African-Americans who charged their passengers the exact amount it cost to ride the bus, carpooling with friends and relatives, or walking to their destinations.

The boycott lasted 381 days. Buses stood idle, and it cost Montgomery approximately $3,000 per day in revenue until the city repealed its law requiring racial segregation on public buses following the United States Supreme Court ruling in a separate court case, wherein it deemed segregation unconstitutional. Rosa Parks was a catalyst in changing the law.

Rosa Parks died of natural causes on October 24, 2005. At age 92, she had endured many hardships, both financial and loss of loved ones, beyond her publicized arrest. After her funeral, her casket was transported to Washington, DC, aboard a bus resembling the one in which she made her protest. She was the first woman and the second black person to lie in honor in the rotunda of the United States Capitol. An estimated 50,000 people viewed the televised event.

Today, Rosa Parks Day is a holiday celebrated in honor of her courage and the tenacity it took to stand up for what she believed in—her rights as a human being and as an American citizen. In California and Missouri, she is honored on her birthday, and in Ohio and Oregon, she is remembered on the day the Montgomery, Alabama, police arrested her on December 1.

—— A ——

I was fortunate enough to be honored at an event in Washington, DC, at the Kennedy Center. My enduring memory of that night is not the award I received nor the two past presidents or sitting vice-president who attended. My enduring memory remains getting to meet Rosa Parks. She was a small, very quiet lady with enough personality and dignity to fill the auditorium. She will forever be remembered as standing up for human rights by simply not giving up her seat.

Oftentimes, we don't have to go around the world or face some exotic ordeal to be heroic. We simply need to address the task in front of us and do the right thing.

In her quote, *"I have learned over the years that when one's mind is made up, this diminishes fear,"* Rosa Parks reminds us that fear is a constant part of the human condition. Heroes feel the fear and perform heroically in spite of it. However, she leaves us with a powerful piece of advice. Once we make up our minds to pursue a path, fear takes a back seat.

14

"I have a dream that one day this nation will rise up and live out the true meaning of its creed: We hold these truths to be self-evident, that all men are created equal."

—MARTIN LUTHER KING JR.

ON AUGUST 28, 1963, Martin Luther King Jr. delivered his legendary "I Have a Dream" speech during the March on Washington event before the Lincoln Memorial and an estimated 250,000 demonstrators. It has become one of the most powerful speeches in America.

The March on Washington came on the centennial of the Emancipation Proclamation decreed by President Abraham Lincoln on January 1, 1863, in which he declared that slaves in all confederate states would be "forever free." It was intended to dramatize the racial injustices of African-Americans in the southern states and pressure John F. Kennedy's administration to initiate a federal civil rights bill in Congress.

Martin Luther King Jr. delivered a seventeen-minute speech near the end of the event in which he veered from his prepared remarks and told of his dream for the nation. In it, he said:

> I say to you today, my friends, so even though we face the difficulties of today and tomorrow, I still have a dream. It is a dream deeply rooted in the American dream.

I have a dream that one day this nation will rise up and live out the true meaning of its creed: "We hold these truths to be self-evident: that all men are created equal."

I have a dream that one day on the red hills of Georgia the sons of former slaves and the sons of former slave owners will be able to sit down together at the table of brotherhood.

I have a dream that one day even the state of Mississippi, a state sweltering with the heat of injustice, sweltering with the heat of oppression, will be transformed into an oasis of freedom and justice.

I have a dream that my four little children will one day live in a nation where they will not be judged by the color of their skin but by the content of their character.

I have a dream today.

I have a dream that one day, down in Alabama, with its vicious racists, with its governor having his lips dripping with the words of interposition and nullification; one day right there in Alabama, little black boys and black girls will be able to join hands with little white boys and white girls as sisters and brothers.

I have a dream today.

Following the event, Martin Luther King Jr. commented, "As television beamed the image of this extraordinary gathering across the border oceans, everyone who believed in man's capacity to better himself had a moment of inspiration and confidence in the future of the human race."

Approximately eight months later, on April 3, 1968, Martin Luther King Jr. delivered his last speech, "I've Been to the Mountaintop," before the Mason Temple in Memphis, Tennessee. His message called for unity, economic actions, boycotts, and nonviolent protests concerning the Memphis sanitation strike. At the end of his speech, he spoke of seeing the Promised Land and of his fear of no man. The next day, as he stood on the second-floor balcony of his room at the Lorraine Motel in Memphis, Tennessee, Martin Luther King Jr. was fatally shot.

Though many states observed Martin Luther King Jr.'s contribution to righting the wrongs of racial injustices, for the first time in 1971, on November 2, 1983, President Ronald Reagan signed a bill proclaiming January 20 a federal holiday in King's honor. President George H. W. Bush modified the date to be observed the third Monday of January, coinciding near Martin Luther King Jr.'s birthday on January 15. Gradually, Martin Luther King Jr. Day became observed nationwide. It has also been termed Human Rights Day by some states.

— A —

As a professional speaker, I have long collected recordings of some of the greatest speeches ever made. Martin Luther King Jr.'s "I Have a Dream" speech is among the most powerful and poignant presentations I have ever heard. We now know that he had other remarks prepared that did not include the "I Have a Dream" part of his speech, but as any great speaker or thought leader will do, he recognized the power of the moment and he seized it. Our creed, as Martin Luther King Jr. described it, may never be fully attained, but it will forever be worth striving toward.

Martin Luther King Jr. will forever hold a powerful place in history having changed the way we look at the world. This is significant for anyone, but particularly for a man who was cut down in the prime of his life and who never saw his 40th birthday. His remaining legacy continues to be the dream he had that he shared with us and with future generations of freedom-loving people.

15

*"It has been my experience that folks
who have no vices have very few virtues."*

—ABRAHAM LINCOLN

ABRAHAM LINCOLN, our 16th president of the United States, will be remembered for his integrity rather than his shortcomings. He was determined to make his mark on the world and was committed to the principles set by our country's founders. He dedicated himself to upholding liberty and equality for all. His presidency brought forth changes in America that put an end to slavery.

As a young man growing up on a farm in southern Indiana and Kentucky, he developed a mindset that he would overcome the drudgery of physical labor associated with farm life through self-improvement and ambition. He spent much of his time reading, scribing, writing, ciphering, and writing poetry. Although he attended school as his farm chores allowed, he was largely self-educated. On occasion, he took advantage of the schooling offered by traveling teachers who tutored students as they moved from town to town.

Abraham Lincoln received his law license on September 9, 1836. He had become an attorney and counselor of law without attending law school or passing the bar examination. Instead, he was considered to have "good moral character" by the Illinois Supreme Court. During his nearly twenty-five years in practice, he represented many civil and criminal actions, including debt, slander, divorce, endowment and apportionment, mortgage foreclosures, and murder.

His legal reputation gave rise to the nickname "Honest Abe" in a profession that he admitted had a "popular belief that lawyers are necessarily dishonest." He, undoubtedly, earned his nickname while working as a young store clerk in Salem, Illinois. It has been reported that when he realized a customer was shortchanged, even by a small amount of money, he closed the store and delivered the correct change in person, no matter how far the walk. His advice to potential young lawyers was, "Resolve to be honest at all events; and if in your judgment you cannot be an honest lawyer, resolve to be honest without being a lawyer. Choose some other occupation, rather than one in the choosing of which you do, in advance, consent to be a knave."

Abraham Lincoln said he practiced "every kind of business that could come before a prairie lawyer." His practice included patents filed in the United States, such as the one he received for the flotation device he invented for the movement of boats in shallow water. After being temporarily stranded on a flatboat that came upon a sandbar, Abraham Lincoln began to imagine a device that would lift vessels over river obstructions. Eventually, he designed such a device, and on May 22, 1849, he received Patent No. 6469, although his idea was never commercialized. There has never been another United States president to hold a patent.

In addition to civil cases, Abraham Lincoln defended criminal cases. He represented William "Duff" Armstrong, who went on trial for the murder of James Preston Metzker. Duff Armstrong was acquitted when his attorney, Abraham Lincoln, challenged the testimony and undermined the creditability of a witness's ability to see the incident in the light of the moon by producing the *Farmer's Almanac*, which proved that there was no moon on the night in question.

Abraham Lincoln was not without vices, but he believed that those who were concerned about the flaws of others generally did not positively lend to society.

———— A ————

Abraham Lincoln will remain a towering historical figure in the history of the United States, and the world, as he will be remembered for healing our divided country and restoring our Union. When I think of his quote regarding vices and virtues, it always reminds me that none of us is perfect. Therefore, groups, organizations, and countries can never achieve perfection. In the preamble to the United States Constitution, it indicates that we will strive to achieve a "more perfect union." The fact that our founders directed us toward being "more perfect" clarifies that it is a wonderful ideal that will never be fully reached.

We have a tendency in our world today to be hypercritical of vices in other people's lives while ignoring their overriding virtues and the contributions they may be making to our world. Like Abraham Lincoln, I am much more interested in the fact that someone reached the mountaintop than how many times someone may have stumbled along the way.

16

"Some men see things as they are, and ask, 'Why?'
I dream of things that never were, and say, 'Why not?'"

—ROBERT FRANCIS KENNEDY

EVER IN HISTORY, was there a time of peace on Earth? Perhaps the reason may be summed up in the words of Robert "Bobby" Kennedy, which he borrowed from Irish playwright George Bernard Shaw: "Some men see things as they are and ask, 'Why?'" This question has caused countless people over endless generations to search for alternatives to the status quo and to dream of something better. Through the pursuit of those dreams, so many lives have been lost.

Bobby Kennedy was born November 20, 1925, in Brookline, Massachusetts, and held public offices after serving in World War II. He became U.S. attorney general, advisor to President John F. Kennedy, his older brother, until his assassination, merely two days shy of Bobby's 38th birthday, and U.S. senator representing the State of Massachusetts.

Robert F. Kennedy was gunned down senselessly before the nation like his brother. On June 5, 1968, he was on the campaign trail delivering his California Primary victory speech in the ballroom of the Embassy Hotel in Los Angeles when 24-year-old Sirhan Sirhan shot him several times. He died the next day. Bobby Kennedy perished, promoting national unity in the wake of Martin Luther King Jr.'s assassination. His message:

What we need in the United States is not division;
what we need in the United States is not hatred;
what we need in the United States is not violence or
lawlessness, but his love and wisdom, and compassion
toward one another.

In his "*Remarks at the University*" *of Kansas* speech on March 18, 1968, Bobby Kennedy addressed its student body, speaking of more that could be done on our soil, as well as around the world. He was specifically addressing the situation in Vietnam in the time of war. He knew that we could do better and felt that the American people agreed.

Bobby Kennedy's funeral was held in New York City's St. Patrick Cathedral among thousands of grief-stricken mourners who crowded the streets waiting for their turns to stroll past his coffin to pay their respects. Five thousand per hour passed his flag-draped coffin. His younger brother, Edward "Ted" Moore Kennedy, concluded his eulogy with this quote that Bobby Kennedy so often recited, for it was what he stood for in life: "Some men see things as they are, and ask, 'Why?' I dream of things that never were, and say, 'Why not?'"

———— A ————

I first became aware of Robert Kennedy the summer I was 9 years old. I was in the hospital for a couple of days having my tonsils removed, and my doctor—trying to put a good spin on the procedure—had told me that I could eat all the ice cream I wanted and watch whatever I chose on television. Unfortunately, after having my tonsils removed, I didn't feel like eating any ice cream, and because Robert Kennedy was shot and subsequently died the following day, there was nothing on the three TV channels that were available at that time other than around-the-clock coverage of the assassination. I remember asking one of the nurses why Mr. Kennedy had been killed. She told me, "Someday you'll be older and you will understand all of this."

Over half a century has come and gone since that time and, while I am indeed older, I have no more clarity or understanding of why promising influential leaders like Robert F. Kennedy have their lives cut tragically short. His quote will live on as a lasting legacy reminding us that, as we look at the world, we can choose to either see problems or see possibilities.

17

"They may forget what you said, but they will never forget how you made them feel."

—MAYA ANGELOU

MARGUERITE ANNIE JOHNSON was born in St. Louis, Missouri, on April 4, 1928. She will forever be admired as a poet, writer, memoirist, civil rights activist, singer, dancer, actress in movies and television, director, producer of plays, movies, and public television programs—a career that spanned over fifty years. She wrote and published seven autobiographies, three books of essays, and poetry.

She took the professional name Maya Angelou early in her career. She combined her childhood nickname given by her beloved older brother, Bailey, who spoke with a stutter and was unable to pronounce her name correctly, referring to her as "Mya Sister," which was later shortened to "Maya," along with a modified version of her former husband's name. Her marriage to Greek sailor Tosh Angelos in 1951 lasted no more than three years, reportedly due to her powerful religious beliefs not shared by her husband, but her career thrived.

Maya Angelou's start in life held a series of misfortunes, including her parents' divorce, various moves to different states to live with relatives, and unspeakable abuses by her mother's boyfriend that she suffered at the age of 8. When she reported the abuse, the man was found guilty. He was jailed for but a day. Four days after his release, he was beaten to death.

Maya Angelou believed his murder to be her fault, and she became mute for nearly five years. "I thought my voice killed him; I killed that man because I told his name. And then I thought I would never speak again because my voice would kill anyone," she recalled. In her first of seven biographies titled, *I Know Why the Caged Bird Sings* (1969), Maya Angelou recounted her life story, up to the age of 17. This remarkable work brought her international recognition and acclaim.

During her time of silence, Maya Angelou developed her exceptional memory, her fondness for literature, and her sense of the world around her. Ultimately, she spoke again with the help of her teacher and friend, Bertha Flowers, who opened her mind up to a new world of poetry by saying, "You do not love poetry—not until you speak it." Maya Angelou was inspired, and she was honored with the invitation to read her most famous poem, "On the Pulse of Morning," at President Bill Clinton's 1993 inauguration. She was the second poet in history asked to deliver her respected work at an inauguration since John F. Kennedy's oath of office in 1961, in which poet and playwright, Robert Frost, recited "The Gift Outright," from memory. The glare of the sun prevented him from reading, "Dedication," a poem he wrote specifically for the occasion.

Maya Angelou wrote about her life with great honesty. She once said that she had no skeletons in her closet—that she had no closets. The openness of her words and her ability to move people's souls brought out the emotions within her readers. They may not remember her exact words, but they remember how she made them feel. Maya Angelou wrote four books in the last ten years of her life while in constant pain in her body due to her dancing career and her respiratory difficulties. She died the morning of May 28, 2014, at 86.

——— A ———

I have written more than fifty books and more than a thousand weekly syndicated columns. Some of the most difficult but rewarding writing I've ever done involves poetry. Poetry takes our thoughts and ideas and delivers them utilizing the words as an art form. Few people ever did this as well as Dr. Maya Angelou.

She reminds us that our words go beyond conveying facts or knowledge. They create emotions and feelings. The highest and best use of our language is to connect with another person's emotions and leave them with positive, uplifting feelings. If you want to experience this, read some of Maya Angelou's poetry, or better yet, find one of the recordings of her reciting her own work.

18

"There are always three speeches, for every one you actually gave. The one you practiced, the one you gave, and the one you wish you gave."

—DALE CARNEGIE

DALE HARBISON CARNAGEY was born in poverty in Maryville, Missouri, on November 24, 1888, and became a pioneer in the professional and human performance movement. Dale Carnegie has influenced individuals, teams, and entire organizations with more than three thousand trainers and consultants and two hundred training offices in more than eighty countries. His training courses have benefited tens of thousands of companies and over eight million individuals worldwide. He developed much of the skills his organization teaches while selling correspondence courses to ranchers and working for Armour & Company selling bacon, soap, and lard. In his employment with the company, he was so successful in his South Omaha, Nebraska, sales territory that he became a national leader.

Dale Carnegie enjoyed speaking in public from an early age and joined his high school's debate team. He became a skillful orator. While attending school, he became intrigued with the Chautauqua lecture circuit. It was an adult organization that brought entertainment and culture to communities through speakers, teachers, musicians, showmen, and preachers who addressed audiences. Instead of joining the assembly after high school, though, he enrolled in the American Academy of Dramatic Arts in New York. There, he found little success as an actor, although it is reported that he played the role of Dr. Hartley in the *Polly of the Circus* roadshow.

When the play ended in 1912, Dale Carnegie took a room at the YMCA in New York and came up with the notion to teach public speaking. He convinced the manager to permit him to hold classes within the facility in exchange for 80 percent of the proceeds. During his first session, he ran out of material and began improvisation. He asked his students to speak to the class about "something that made them angry." This technique was successful in helping them to overcome their fear of addressing audiences. The Dale Carnegie Course evolved, and strong interest arose for people who wanted more self-confidence.

In 1916, Dale Carnegie presented his lecture at Carnegie Hall. The event was a sell-out; and in 1919, he believed that he would be best remembered by changing the spelling of his name in honor of the steel magnate, Andrew Carnegie.

Dale Carnegie's methods include a series of keys to success, including memorization, public speaking, developing greater self-confidence, strengthening people skills, enhancing communications skills, improving attitudes, and developing communications and leadership skills. The course encourages students to take a chance, be enthusiastic, love their work, learn from their mistakes, do not fear "fear," and learn to prioritize.

To his credit, Dale Carnegie wrote many books, including his 1936 bestseller, *How to Win Friends and Influence People*, which has sold more than fifteen million copies worldwide. Other popular books include *How to Stop Worrying and Start Living* (1948) and *Lincoln the Unknown* (1932), which is often presented as a popular award for excellence. In addition, his organization produces numerous booklets and manuals that are distributed to students of the Dale Carnegie & Associates courses.

Dale Carnegie lost his battle with Hodgkin's disease at his home in Forest Hills, New York, on November 1, 1955. Upon his death, his wife, Dorothy Price Vanderpool, took over the company on behalf of her husband. Today, Dale Carnegie & Associates is spearheaded by Joseph K. Hart Jr., president and CEO.

—— A ——

As a professional speaker, I have spoken to well over a million people in arenas, convention centers, and corporate events. Speaking in public is among the greatest fears of most people. I believe that sincerity and spontaneity are the keys to a great speech. The closer you can come to speaking as if you're passing a friend on the street or talking to a neighbor over the fence, the better your speech will be and the more of your message will be received.

Success in most areas of life, including public speaking, comes when we remember it's not about us—it's about our audience and how we can impact their lives. It's much better to have our audience be able to relate to our message and internalize it in their lives than to impress them with our oratory. Remembering that we can never give a perfect speech allows us to do our best and relax in the certain knowledge that our best effort is good enough.

19

"We think sometimes that poverty is only being hungry, naked, and homeless. The poverty of being unwanted, unloved, and uncared for is the greatest poverty."

—SAINT MOTHER TERESA

BEFORE SHE BECAME SAINT MOTHER TERESA, known worldwide for her humanitarian work, she was Agnes (Anjezë) Gonxha Bojaxhiu. Born on August 26, 1910, Agnes was the youngest of three siblings of Albanian descent in Skopje, Macedonia. Her father was a successful merchant, and together with her mother, Drana, older brother Lazar, and sister, Aga, she enjoyed a prosperous childhood. When she was nearly 8 years old, however, her father suddenly died, reportedly in the Balkan ethnic brawl. His absence left the family with economic difficulty.

Nonetheless, her mother raised the family in a loving home, and keeping with their strong Catholic beliefs instilled a sense of generosity and charity in her children through her actions. It was reported that her mother would invite the city's poor to dinner to share nourishment. Her advice to her daughter, "My child, never eat a single mouthful unless you are sharing it with others."

Her mother's influence, and her Jesuit parish of the Sacred Heart, guided Agnes' decision to someday become a missionary. She felt the calling to devote herself to a holy life. That strong desire came at the age of 12. Thus, at age 18, she left her family home to join the Sisters of Loreto, an Irish community of nuns, which had missions in India. There, she received the name Sister Mary Teresa, taking her namesake from Saint Therese of Lisieux, patron saint of missionaries.

One year later, in 1929, she moved to Darjeeling next to the Himalayan Mountains and taught at St. Teresa's School. She took her initial vows as a nun on May 24, 1931. From there, and for the next fifteen years, she taught geography and catechism at St. Mary's in Calcutta. It was an all-girls high school attended by rich children. Her heart went out to the people living in poverty outside the school gates. She later explained, "I was to leave the convent and help the poor while living among them. It was an order. To fail would have been to break the faith."

On May 24, 1937, she made her Final Profession of Vows, becoming "the spouse of Jesus" for "all eternity," she said. Sister Teresa took the name, "Mother" Teresa, a customary title to the sisters in her order. At that moment, she committed to a life of poverty, chastity, and obedience.

Mother Teresa founded a new religious congregation for Catholic nuns in 1950. Approved by the pope, she named it the Missionaries of Charity, and its congregation ran an open-air school for the poor. Today, it has become a global organization with thousands of volunteers in over 130 countries. In 1952, she opened the first Home for the Dying in Calcutta.

Mother Teresa spent her life making people who were hungry, naked, and homeless feel cared for, wanted, and loved. For her generosity and work with the poor of the world, Mother Teresa won countless awards and honors, including the Nobel Peace Prize in 1979, "for work undertaken in the struggle to overcome poverty and distress, which also constitutes a threat to peace." Rather than holding the traditional celebratory award banquet, Mother Teresa requested that the $192,000 budget be reallocated and donated to the poor of India.

Mother Teresa died on September 5, 1997, just nine days after her 87th birthday.

In March 2016, Pope Francis selected Mother Teresa to be canonized after "verifying" two miracles she performed. Vatican law states that the initial miracle attributed to a candidate for sainthood means beautification can be conferred. When a second miracle occurs, canonization and entry into sainthood can occur.

Mother Teresa's first miracle was verified in 2003 under Pope John Paul II's papacy. In 1998, a woman from India was cured of a fatal abdominal tumor when she placed a medallion on her abdomen that Mother Teresa had held in her hand. The next day, the tumor was gone. The second miracle was verified in 2015 under Pope Francis. In 2008, a Brazilian man was cured of a brain abscess after his wife put a relic on his head and recited the prayer of beautification and heartfelt prayer to Mother Teresa. Miraculously, the man woke from his coma and made a rapid and total recovery. His wife's prayers had been answered.

On September 4, 2016, at St. Peter's Square, Vatican City State, Rome, Mother Teresa officially entered the hallowed halls of sainthood. She became known as Saint Mother Teresa.

Saint Mother Teresa is one of only eight people to be granted honorary citizenship in the United States. People speak of kindness and compassion, but Mother Teresa devoted her life to serving others with kindness and compassion.

Throughout my career as an author, speaker, movie producer, and entrepreneur, I've been humbled to receive a number of awards and honors, but none more humbling than when I was recognized as the International Humanitarian of the Year. The impact of that occasion became extremely real to me when I learned that the previous recipient of the honor had been Saint Mother Teresa. I began studying about her work and her life, so that I could pay tribute to her during my remarks after receiving the award.

While she certainly left us with some powerful words expressing her thoughts, ideas, and faith, her actions spoke louder than any of her words and continues to impact our world today. In our society, unfortunately, when it's all said and done, too often there's more said than done. But then, a simple, quiet, and humble person like Saint Mother Teresa comes along to show us the way.

20

"You must be the change you wish to see in the world."

—MAHATMA GANDHI

MOHANDAS KARAMCHAND GANDHI, known to the world as Mahatma Gandhi, was born to a Hindu family in coastal Gujarat, India. He became an Indian lawyer, anti-colonial nationalist, and political ethicist who channeled his existence to promote nonviolent resistance and led the campaign for India's independence from British rule. His movement inspired civil rights and freedom around the world. He came to be in October 1869 and was first honored with the title Mahatma, meaning "great soul," in 1914 in South Africa. In modern English, its meaning is likened to the term "saint."

At age 9, Gandhi entered the local school near his home, where he studied the basics of arithmetic, history, geography, and the Gujarati language. When he was 11, he joined the high school. He was a shy, tongue-tied average student, who had no attraction for play or games; his only interests were books and school lessons.

When Gandhi was 13 years old, he married 14-year-old Kasturbai Kapadia, affectionately called Ba, in an arranged marriage, according to custom. He, his brother, and his cousin were all married simultaneously. Recalling the day of the wedding, he said, "As we didn't know much about marriage, for us it meant only wearing new clothes, eating sweets, and playing with relatives." He went on to have a successful marriage—for sixty-two years—which produced four sons, Harilal, Manilal, Ramdas, and Devdas.

Gandhi studied law at the Inner Temple in London, and in June 1891 he became a lawyer. He was 22 years old when he attempted his law practice. Unfortunately, his efforts failed, so he moved to South Africa to represent an Indian merchant in a lawsuit at the request of his cousin. The case brought him to South Africa in May 1894, but his fight against discrimination against the Indians in South Africa kept him there for twenty-one years. And it was there that he developed his political views and strong ethics. From his political power, he helped found the Natal Indian Congress, and he continued his fight against the injustices of his people for the remainder of his life.

Significantly influenced by his mother, who was an extremely pious woman, it was said that she "would not think of taking her meals without her daily prayers—she would take the hardest vows and keep them without flinching. To keep two or three consecutive fasts was nothing to her." Gandhi, too, practiced asceticism and used nutritional abstinence as a political tool. He often threatened suicide unless demands were met. His fasts were highly publicized and generated widespread sympathy.

As Gandhi grew older, his lifestyle was characterized by self-denial from sensual pleasures, pursuing spiritual goals, and reflecting on spirituality and religious matters in the tradition of Buddhism and Hinduism. He chose to live a frugal lifestyle.

On September 22, 1921, Mahatma Gandhi made a meaningful decision to abandon his elaborate Gujarati dress style. Instead, he chose a simple dhoti or loincloth and shawl to express compassion for the poor of India.

At 78 years of age, Mahatma Gandhi was assassinated by a Hindu nationalist on January 30, 1948, in the compound of

Birla House, which was a large mansion in central New Delhi. Today, it is a museum dedicated to his honor.

Shortly before Gandhi's assassination, he gave his grandson, Arun, a handwritten paper with a list of the Seven Sins, as he defined them: Wealth without work; Pleasure without conscience; Knowledge without character; Commerce without morality; Science without humanity; Religion without sacrifice; and Politics without principle.

Announcing his death, Indian independence activist and then Prime Minister Jawaharlal Nehru addressed his countrymen over the national public radio broadcast of India and reported the passing of Mahatma Gandhi, saying:

> Friends and comrades, the light has gone out of our lives, and there is darkness everywhere, and I do not quite know what to tell you or how to say it. Our beloved leader, Bapu, as we called him, the father of the nation, is no more. Perhaps I am wrong to say that; nevertheless, we will not see him again, as we have seen him for these many years, we will not run to him for advice or seek solace from him, and that is a terrible blow, not only for me but for millions and millions in this country.

Gandhi's four sons, like their father, were committed to the Indian independence movement. They, too, faced multiple imprisonments throughout their lives. It was his third son, Ramdas, whom he requested to light the fire to start his cremation.

Mahatma Gandhi did not receive the Nobel Peace Prize, although he was nominated five times. However, the government of India awards the annual Gandhi Peace Prize to distinguished social workers, world leaders, and citizens.

In 2011, *Time* magazine named Gandhi one of the top twenty-five political icons of all time. He was the change he wished for the world.

Gandhi's quote stands as a reminder to us all that the only person in the world we can change is ourselves, and the only part of our lives we can control is our efforts and our attitudes. My academic background is in the field of psychology and sociology. One of the most powerful tools that can be utilized in couples, family, or group counseling is to ask each individual, "Are you willing to undertake this process and do the work if you are the only person who changes?"

It's easy to be skeptical in our world today when people use the media to speak one way, and then it is revealed that they act and live another way. I believe we can change the world one person at a time, but the one person we have to change is ourselves. Laws in a civilized society are based upon the principle flowing out of the question, "What if everyone acted exactly like you?"

21

"*Everybody is a genius. But if you judge a fish by its ability to climb a tree, it will live its whole life believing that it is stupid.*"

—ALBERT EINSTEIN

ALBERT EINSTEIN was born on March 14, 1879. Known simply as "Einstein," he was born in Germany and was considered the most outstanding physicist of all time. He was primarily best known for developing the "theory of relativity" and made significant contributions to developing the "theory of quantum mechanics," among other theories and accomplishments. His intellectual achievements and exceptional natural capabilities earned him the distinction of being a "genius," defined as having an extraordinarily high Intelligence Quotient (IQ) rating, typically above 140. Einstein's IQ was reportedly 160. Customarily, a score of 135 or above puts a person in the 99th percentile of the population.

As a youth, Einstein outshined in mathematics and physics well ahead of his peers. He taught himself algebra and geometry over one summer. After giving him a geometry textbook to read, his family tutor, Max Talmud, said of the 12-year-old, "[Einstein] had worked through the whole book. He thereupon devoted himself to higher mathematics…Soon the flight of his mathematical genius was so high I could not follow."

CHAPTER 21

At 13, Einstein became more interested in music. In his late journals, he wrote: "If I were not a physicist, I would probably be a musician. I often think in music. I live my daydreams in music. I see my life in terms of music…I get most joy in life out of music."

His mother, Pauline, was very well educated and a quiet woman with an affection for the arts. She played the piano in her spare time. When Einstein was 5 years old, she made her son begin violin lessons, but at such an early age, he did not enjoy it. Throughout his life, especially in school, Einstein battled authority and resented the school's regimen and teaching methods. He later wrote, "The spirit of learning and creative thought was lost in strict rote learning." This proved true for him in the process of learning to play the violin.

At age 13, though, his appreciation for the instrument was rejuvenated when he heard the violin sonatas of Mozart. He became captivated by Mozart's composition and continued his study of music. Einstein taught himself to play without "ever practicing systematically." He said that "love is a better teacher than a sense of duty."

At 17, a school examiner heard Einstein playing Beethoven's violin sonatas. The examiner stated afterward that his playing was "remarkable and revealing of 'great insight.'" He displayed a deep love of music. It played an important and permanent part in Einstein's life, proving that being passionate about something and using that passion as a catalyst to perfection can make anyone a genius to their craft. Even though the idea of becoming a professional musician was not on his mind, he continued to perform on the violin for private audiences and friends.

Albert Einstein died from an abdominal aortic aneurysm on April 18, 1955. He requested that his body be cremated; but in an outlandish twist, a Princeton pathologist, Thomas Harvey, removed his brain during the autopsy and kept it for future research, hoping to discover the key to his genius. In 1999, a Canadian university team published a controversial paper claiming that Einstein possessed unusual folds on his parietal lobe, a part of the brain associated with mathematical and spatial ability.

During his illness, Einstein refused surgery, saying, "I want to go when I want. It is tasteless to prolong life artificially. I have done my share; it is time to go. I will go elegantly." Albert Einstein continued his work until the end of his life at age 76.

———— A ————

Einstein reminds us of the simple truth that if we're going to win in life, we have to play to our strengths. All of us have talents and gifts that make certain activities easy, fun, and productive for us. As a young man, I was the national Olympic weightlifting champion. As a competitive weightlifter, all of your training makes you very strong within a very narrow groove or range of motion. If you get even a fraction of an inch outside of that power groove, your world-class strength can become very ordinary.

Michael Jordon was arguably the greatest basketball player of all time. But when, in his prime, he decided to play baseball, he proved to be only a mediocre Minor League Baseball player. In my novel and subsequent movie, *The Ultimate Gift*, I built on the theme that we find meaning in life when we discover our gifts, but we find significance when we give our gifts to the world.

22

*"A life spent making mistakes is not only more honorable,
but more useful than a life spent doing nothing."*

—GEORGE BERNARD SHAW

GEORGE BERNARD SHAW was born in a lower-middle-class community in Dublin, Ireland, on July 26, 1856, to George Carr Shaw and Lucinda Elizabeth (Gurly). At his insistence, he was also known as simply Bernard Shaw. Early in his life, he experienced family trouble coming from a broken home. He, his mother, and his siblings escaped "shabby-genteel poverty," as he termed his lifestyle with his father. He pondered whether his mother's close friend, George John Lee, a well-known Dublin conductor and vocal instructor, was his biological father. His theory was based on her relationship with him at George Bernard Shaw's birth. Nonetheless, Lee played a significant role in his life, and his home was often brimming with music and laughter with frequent gatherings of singers and musicians.

In 1876, at age 20, George Bernard Shaw moved to London. He struggled to establish himself as a writer and novelist, and publishers repeatedly rejected his works. He believed himself to be a failure writing novels and began writing plays. It was then that he began a disciplined process of self-education.

By the mid-1880s, Shaw found success as a playwright and established himself as a well-known, respected theatre and music critic. His witty style, combining both contemporary satire and historical storytelling, established him as a genius playwright, leading dramatist, and social commentator of his generation. Of his sixty plays, perhaps his most notable were *Arms & the Man* and *Pygmalion*, which was later made into the movie, renamed *My Fair Lady*. George Bernard Shaw was the first writer to win both the Nobel Prize for Literature (1925) and an Academy Award for "Best Adapted Screenplay" for *Pygmalion* in 1938.

Shaw professed many strong beliefs throughout his life, including his political views, always favoring a peaceful means over violence. Many of his plays were catalysts to permeating his political and social causes, including women's rights and racial equality, among his audiences.

Often, his beliefs were contradictory and contentious. The Spanish scholar and statesman Salvador de Madariaga described him as "a pole of negative electricity set in a people of positive electricity."

There was one particular facet of George Bernard Shaw's life in which he did not waver. In his writing, he refused to follow traditional English forms of spelling words and punctuating sentences. Consistently, he spelled with variations of words such as "shew" for "show," and he altered the English spelling of words like "honour" and "favour," by dropping the "u" within the word, as is common in American spelling. Shaw also abandoned the apostrophe in contractions, such as "can't," "won't," and "that's," whenever possible.

In 1946, the year of his 90th birthday, the government asked him informally whether he would accept the Order of Merit, a Commonwealth award recognizing distinguished service in the armed forces, science, art, literature, or the promotion of culture. He declined. He believed that "an author's merit would only be determined by a posthumous verdict of history."

CHAPTER 22

George Bernard Shaw continued to write into his nineties. His last plays were *Buoyant Billions* (1947), *Farfetched Fables* (1948), a set of six short plays, *Shakes versus Shay* (1949), a ten-minute piece in which Shakespeare and Shaw trade insults, and *Why She Would Not* (1950), "a little comedy."

In 1906, George Bernard Shaw and his wife of forty-five years, Charlotte Payne-Townshend Shaw, moved into a 3.5-acre estate they called Shaw's Corner. It became their primary residence. Originally, it was built as a rectory for the village at Ayot St. Lawrence in Hertfordshire, England. By the time they moved there, Shaw was already an acclaimed dramatist.

Secluded, at the bottom of his garden, was a home-built revolving hut he labeled as "London," where he was known to have written many of his major works. It was a small 5'9" square structure constructed on a central steel-pole frame with a circular track designed so that he could rotate the building on its axis to follow the arc of the sun's light throughout the day. It was named such that unwanted visitors could be informed that he was away "visiting the capital."

Today, visitors from all around the world walk the grounds and visit the estate to view the author's "hut" in its original state. Perched on his desk is an antique Remington Portable Typewriter, alongside his eyeglasses, and a vintage black telephone is mounted on the wall next to his desk. His writings are gone from the hut, but his spirit lives on within the compound.

After Charlotte died in 1943, she was cremated. Shaw spent the rest of his life in quiet solitude. His loss was more deeply felt than he had ever imagined, for, throughout his life, he prided himself on indifference in all loss and misfortune.

George Bernard Shaw died in his dining room on November 2, 1950, at 94 from renal failure. His ashes were mixed with his wife's, and their ashes were scattered along the footpaths of the classic English garden he enjoyed tending to and around "Saint Joan," which was a statue in remembrance of George Bernard Shaw's play about the 15th century French military figure Joan of Arc.

In his will, George Bernard Shaw's bequest, after some specific monetary distributions, was that his remaining assets be put in a trust to form a fundamental reform of the English alphabet to be converted into a phonetic version of forty letters. His intentions were precise, but his formulation was flawed, so the courts, initially, ruled the trust void. Later, an out-of-court agreement provided a sum be set aside for spelling reform. Most of the £8,300 was spent on a special phonetic edition of *Androcles and the Lion*, which was published in 1962. It was written in the Shavian alphabet, also known as the Shaw alphabet. It was conceived by Shaw to provide simple, phonemic orthography for the English language and intended to replace the difficulties of conventional spelling. There were three main criteria for the new alphabet: it should be at least forty letters; be as phonetic as possible; it must be distinct from the Latin alphabet to avoid the misconception of being misspelled. The Shavian alphabet did not catch on to become the mainstream.

Among Shaw's wishes, he left instructions in his will that his executor, the Public Trustee, must license publications of his works only under the name Bernard Shaw.

George Bernard Shaw's influence began in the 1880s and continues well beyond his death. He spent a lifetime proving that "doing" leads to success.

George Bernard Shaw was one of the great wordsmiths of all times. His powerful quote reminds us that failure is not the opposite of success—it is part of success. The ability to embrace, learn from, and build on failure is the cornerstone of success.

In our social media world, we have a tendency to judge our own reality against everyone else's highlight reel that they post online. As a writer, I've always been a huge admirer of Ernest Hemingway. The quality of his work seems almost untouchable, but several years ago when one of his books was being republished, they included his first draft of the project in the back of the book. Experiencing Hemingway's first draft would bring hope to any aspiring writer, and it reminds us that failure leads to mediocrity, which leads to progress, that culminates in success.

23

"When one door of happiness closes, another opens, but often we look so long at the closed door that we do not see the one that has been opened for us."

—HELEN KELLER

BORN ON A FARM near Tuscumbia, Alabama, on June 27, 1880, Helen Adams Keller has since been an inspiration to blind, deaf, and mute children and adults worldwide. She will forever be remembered for her courage and grit in overcoming her disabilities and her lifelong mission to help others experience a fulfilling life despite adversities.

When she was 19 months old, the once normal infant was stricken with an illness that her doctor described as brain congestion. She became a wild child, kicking and screaming when she was angry, and giggling and laughing when happy. At the time, Helen Keller was diagnosed as having suffered from either scarlet fever or meningitis. Later, it was thought that she contracted Usher Syndrome, an extremely rare disorder known to be inherited. It is caused by changes or mutations in genes— chemically coded instructions in cells that tell the cells what to do. This affliction robbed her of all sight and hearing.

Helen Keller never disclosed when her mother realized that she was deaf and blind, but she conveyed in her writings that when, as an infant, her mother asked her a question, and she did not respond, she then shouted at her. That is when she realized her daughter could not hear. When she looked into her eyes, she realized she, too, was blind. For the next four years, Helen Keller lived at home with her parents and four siblings, scared, unruly, and shut off from the world.

In time, Helen Keller communicated moderately with the daughter of the family's cook, Martha Washington, who was two years older and understood her signs by the age of 7. By then, she had more than sixty signs that she gestured to communicate with her family, and she could also distinguish various individuals by the vibration of their footsteps.

When she was 6 years old, Helen Keller's mother, Kate, was inspired by what she read in Charles Dickens' *American Notes*. In it, he told of the successful education another blind and deaf woman received. So, accompanied by her father, Captain Arthur Henley Keller, she went to see Dr. J. Julian Chisolm, who was an eye, ear, nose, and throat specialist in Baltimore, Maryland. The physician, then, referred them to Alexander Graham Bell, who had been working with deaf children. He advised the family to contact the Perkins Institute for the Blind in South Boston, Massachusetts.

Accepted into the institute, the school's director asked 20-year-old Anne Sullivan, also visually impaired, to become Helen Keller's instructor. Fourteen years her senior, Anne Sullivan became her governess and companion, and she was constantly by her side. She taught her many methods of communications, including braille, sign language, handwriting, typing, and a method known as Tadoma, in which she placed her hands on a person's face, touching their lips, throat, jaws, and nose to feel vibrations and movements associated with speech.

In addition, she had learned to speak. Though not well understood, she once said, "Longingly, I feel how much more good I could have done if I had acquired normal speech."

Most importantly, Anne Sullivan taught Helen Keller that she could overcome deafblindness.

In 1900, Helen Keller was admitted to the famous Radcliffe College in Cambridge, Massachusetts, graduating in 1904 with a bachelor of arts degree. She became the first deafblind person to earn a bachelor's degree. In her third year, she wrote her autobiography, *The Story of My Life*. In it, she recounted her journey from childhood, with a severe handicap, to her life as a 21-year-old college student.

As an American icon, Helen Keller accomplished many things. With her efforts to improve the treatment of deaf and blind people, she was influential in removing the disabled from asylums, and she prompted the organization of commissions for the blind in thirty states. In 1915, along with American pioneer city planner, George Kessler, she founded the "Helen Keller International" organization, combatting causes and consequences of blindness and malnutrition, including agricultural programs that help families and villages raise nutritious food, which she believed was a major cause of blindness in the world. She campaigned for women's suffrage, those with disabilities, labor rights, and world peace.

Helen Keller authored fourteen books and hundreds of speeches and essays, visited thirty-five countries on five continents, and met world leaders such as Winston Churchill, Golda Meir, and President John F. Kennedy.

Helen Keller has been honored worldwide and has many awards symbolizing her accomplishments and influences. She received honorary doctoral degrees from Temple and Harvard Universities in the United States; Glasgow and Berlin Universities in Europe; Delhi University in India; and Witwatersrand University in South Africa. She also inspired the documentary film *Helen Keller in Her Story*, which received an honorary Academy Award in 1955.

Only a few weeks before her 87th birthday, on June 1, 1968, Helen Keller died in her sleep. She had suffered a series of strokes in 1961 and spent the remainder of her life at her home in Connecticut. At her public memorial service, Senator Lister Hill of Alabama gave a eulogy in which he said, "She will live on, one of the few, the immortal names not born to die. Her spirit will endure as long as man can read, and stories can be told of the woman who showed the world there are no boundaries to courage and faith."

Helen Keller was an inspiration to those who suffer deafblindness, and she taught everyone to forever recognize opportunities for a better life.

As a blind person, myself, I have always thought of Helen Keller as a pioneer and monumental figure. A number of years ago, I met and befriended her great-grandniece, Keller Johnson, who continues to carry the torch and the legacy of her famous ancestor. As a person without sight, I am acutely aware of my dependence on my hearing to navigate the world. In communicating with deaf people, I have learned that they similarly lean on their sight to access information and connect with other people. Helen Keller was both deaf and blind, which multiplies and compounds the challenges faced. Her story was immortalized in the award-winning movie, *The Miracle Worker.*

In her quote, *"When one door of happiness closes, another opens, but often we look so long at the closed door that we do not see the one that has been opened for us,"* Helen Keller reminds us that no single incident or circumstance is either good or bad. We have the right to choose to turn any problem, challenge, or setback into a springboard to something great in the future. In this way, failure becomes fertilizer for our future bountiful harvest.

24

"Most people do not listen with the intent to understand;
they listen with the intent to reply."

—STEPHEN R. COVEY

STEPHEN RICHARDS COVEY was born October 24, 1932, in Salt Lake City, Utah. Though he was a professor, businessman, and keynote speaker to many well-known companies and organizations, he was best known for his book, *The 7 Habits of Highly Effective People*, which has sold more than thirty million copies worldwide. His audio version was the first nonfiction audiobook in the United States publishing history to sell more than a million copies.

First published in 1989, the book offered his approach to being hugely effective at achieving goals by aligning oneself to what he called "true north" principles—permanent and unchanging rules or laws. The Church of Jesus Christ of Latter-day Saints greatly influenced Stephen Covey, and his concepts relied on character ethics, rather than personality ethics. The principles have become universal and timeless. Being an educator at heart, he often taught, "There are three constants in life: change, choice, and principles."

In his book, Covey listed seven habits. One mentioned is to seek first to understand. He sets forth that the most notable life skill is to communicate at all levels of the organization and that listening is essential to understanding. "You spend years learning how to read and write, and years learning how to speak," he said, "But what about listening?"

As a sequel to *The 7 Habits of Highly Effective People*, Stephen Covey published *The 8th Habit: From Effectiveness to Greatness* in 2004. He believed that effectiveness was not enough, saying, "The challenges and complexity we face today are of a different order of magnitude." He strongly advised, "Find your voice and inspire others to find theirs."

Stephen R. Covey and Associates was established in 1985, and two years later, it became the Covey Leadership Center. In 1997, the organization merged with Franklin Quest to form FranklinCovey. Today, the company is a global professional services firm specializing in training and productivity tools for individuals and organizations. His legacy of personal and professional development continues to influence people worldwide.

As a youth, Covey was athletic. Had he not suffered an injury to his hip in junior high school and redirected his attention from athletics to academics, his life may have taken a different path. Stephen Covey earned a bachelor's degree in business administration from the University of Utah, a master's degree in the same field of study from Harvard, and a doctorate from Brigham Young University. In addition, he received ten honorary degrees.

Stephen Covey died on July 16, 2012, at age 79. In April of that year, he rode his bicycle in Rock Canyon Park in Provo, Utah. When he went down a hill too fast, he flipped forward. Losing control, he fell. Although he was wearing a helmet, it slipped, and his head hit the pavement. He left behind his wife, nine children, and fifty-five grandchildren. Throughout his life, he received many awards. Among them was the Fatherhood Award from the National Fatherhood Initiative in 2003.

—— A ——

As the author of more than fifty books, I look back on the early days of my writing career, and I remain grateful for the successful authors who were willing to lend their names to promote one of my books by writing an endorsement. Among the literary luminaries who helped me in the beginning of my career was Dr. Stephen Covey. He was a great writer and teacher. Many successful entrepreneurs, Fortune 500 executives, and world leaders point to profound truths they learned from Stephen Covey.

In Covey's quote, *"Most people do not listen with the intent to understand; they listen with the intent to reply,"* he gives us the secret to turning a monologue into a dialogue. If we are simply talking and not listening, there is no chance we can benefit from the exchange—and little chance we can impact anyone else. But if we listen, we can truly begin to communicate, thereby opening the door to understanding, which is the key to all human growth. Even when we disagree with another person, the simple act of listening gives them the gift of knowing that they have been heard, which makes it more likely they will listen and create an opportunity for a true and lasting connection.

25

"A promise made should be a promise kept."

— STEVE FORBES

MALCOLM STEVENSON "STEVE" FORBES JR. is an American publishing executive, an advisor at the Forbes School of Business & Technology, a prominent public speaker, a politician, a 1996 and 2000 Republican presidential primary election candidate, and the Editor-in-Chief of the high-profile business publication, *Forbes*.

In 1917, Steve Forbes' grandfather, Bertie Charles Forbes, also known as "B.C.," founded *Forbes* magazine. It was the only major business magazine in the United States throughout the 1920s. More than 100 years later, it remains relevant, focusing on people, financial markets, and new ideas and technologies in an ever-changing world.

In 1973, Steve Forbes began writing for *Forbes* under the leadership of his father, Malcolm Forbes. In 1980, he became the president and chief operating officer of the magazine. After his father died in 1990, he became its chief executive officer. Under Steve Forbes' direction, the company has expanded its publishing ventures and has transformed the magazine into an online publishing giant.

Born on July 18, 1947, Steve Forbes graduated cum laude from Brooks School in North Andover, Massachusetts, in 1966. He graduated from Princeton University in 1970, where he founded his first magazine, *Business Today*, along with two other students. The magazine is currently the largest student-run magazine in the world.

In the early morning of April 3, 2016, southbound Amtrak train 89 traveling from New York to Savannah, Georgia, struck a backhoe that obstructed the track in Chester, Pennsylvania, just outside of Philadelphia. The impact extensively damaged its cab, killing two track workers and hospitalizing forty-one passengers. The lead engine had derailed. On his way to Washington, DC, Steve Forbes was among the 337 people on board that day. He was scheduled to participate in the C-SPAN interview program *In Depth*, but did not complete his trip. Fortunately surviving the crash uninjured, he joined the interview by telephone and relayed his experience that morning. He later said, "It was abrupt, so everyone's coffee flew through the air. Everyone knew that this was not your normal slow down or stop."

In 1971, Steve Forbes married Sabina Beekman. They have five daughters, including Moira Forbes, who has followed in her father's footsteps. She is currently the chief executive of Forbes Media LLC.

After I was selected by the President's Committee on Equal Opportunity as the *Entrepreneur of the Year*, I was contacted by Steve Forbes and asked to be one of the twelve people featured in the Forbes book, *Great Success Stories: Twelve Tales of Victory Wrested from Defeat*. I was grateful to be included in that project because, among other things, it was the beginning of my personal and professional relationship with Steve Forbes. He has been gracious enough to endorse several of my books, share the stage with me at speaking engagements, and even appear in a cameo role—playing himself—in our movie, *The Lamp*, based on my novel of the same name. Whenever my schedule takes me anywhere near New York City, I contact Mr. Forbes to see if he can spare some time for a meeting. I've spent many enjoyable days conversing with him in the library built by his father, Malcolm Forbes, in the Forbes building.

No name is more synonymous with capitalism, success, or entrepreneurship than that of Forbes. As in most of his profound statements, Steve Forbes' quote goes far beyond money, contracts, or commerce. It extends to the heart of integrity in our human experience.

26

*"It is amazing what you can accomplish if
you do not care who gets the credit."*

—HARRY S. TRUMAN

HARRY S. TRUMAN was born in Lamar, Missouri, on May 8, 1884. The farm boy from Missouri grew up to become the 33rd president of the United States. On June 10, 1948, during the presidential election campaign, he delivered a speech at the grand Elks Temple in Bremerton, Washington, striking out against his opponent. Though there is some debate about what was truly said, history recalls that an enthusiastic supporter in the crowd hollered out, "Give 'em hell, Harry!" He responded, "I don't give them hell. I just tell the truth about them, and they think it's hell." From that day forward, Harry Truman was forever known as "Give 'em hell, Harry." It was not known or remembered, perhaps, who it was that tagged him with the nickname that day, but it became his lifelong slogan among his supporters.

When the United States entered World War I in 1917, Harry Truman enlisted in the Missouri National Guard after being rejected by the United States Military Academy at West Point in New York due to his poor eyesight. He received his commission as a first lieutenant, Battery F, 2nd Field Artillery Regiment, and his unit was deployed to France on September 5.

Truman's wartime experiences had progressively transformed him from a family farmer to a decorated colonel in the United

States Army with the fortitude to motivate and direct others. War had proven him a leader, and his highly developed leadership qualities became an asset in his post-war political career. Although, his interest in politics had initially been sparked earlier by his first political position in 1900 when he worked as a page at the Democratic National Convention in Kansas City.

After Harry Truman returned from the war, for which he was awarded a World War I Victory Medal, two battle clasps signifying the campaigns he served, a Defense Sector clasp, and two Armed Forces Reserve Medals, he returned to Kansas City, Missouri. He was ready to marry his long-time sweetheart, Bess Wallace, whom he had asked to wait for him until he returned from the war, saying, "I don't think it would be right for me to ask you to tie yourself to a prospective cripple—or a sentiment." They were married on June 18, 1919, and four years later, they had their only child, Mary Margaret. That same year, he and his war-time buddy, Edward "Eddie" Jacobson, opened the Truman and Jacobson Haberdashery. When the haberdashery fell on hard times in 1921, only two years after it opened, he decided to further his political career. He became the senator from Missouri.

When World War II broke out in 1939, Truman was anxious to resume his military service, but there were barriers, including his age—he was 55 years old. Then-President Franklin D. Roosevelt was adamant that senators and congressmen who belonged to the military reserve support the war efforts by remaining in Congress and ending their active duty. Thus, Truman abandoned the notion of returning to military service.

Harry S. Truman was destined to serve as leader of the free world. Elected vice president of the United States under Franklin D. Roosevelt's presidency, he was sworn in on January 20, 1945. Only eighty-two days into his fourth term in office,

Franklin Roosevelt died, and Harry Truman became president of the United States, finishing the term. He continued his service when he was elected president from 1949 to 1953.

Among his accomplishments while in office, Harry Truman implemented the Marshall Plan to rebuild the post-war economy in Europe; established the Truman Doctrine intended to contain the spread of communism in America, which led to his 1949 signing of the North American Treaty Organization (NATO); and in 1950, he announced that the United States would develop a hydrogen bomb. Two-and-a-half years later, the bomb was tested at Eniwetok Atoll in the South Pacific.

Harry Truman defended his decision by saying:

As President of the United States, I had the fateful responsibility of deciding whether or not to use this weapon for the first time. It was the hardest decision I ever had to make. But the President cannot duck hard problems—he cannot pass the buck. I made the decision after discussions with the ablest men in our Government, and after long and prayerful consideration, I decided that the bomb should be used in order to end the war quickly and save countless lives—Japanese as well as American.

Harry Truman also faced the decay of the White House. In 1948, contractors realized the need for major structural repairs when a leg of Mary Margaret's piano fell through her second-floor sitting room and lodged through the ceiling of the family dining room below. Due to many disasters, such as its burning in the War of 1812, fire to the West Wing in 1929, previous presidential renovations ignoring structural requirements, and

156 years of erosion due to old age, the mansion was rapidly crumbling. The demolition and restoration were completed in 1952. In the meantime, the president and his family took up residency at the Blair House—guesthouse to visiting dignitaries.

On November 1, 1950, while Harry Truman napped after lunch, two politically driven Puerto Rican nationalists attempted to enter the Blair House with assassination in mind. They strolled to the door and opened fire. The incident was foiled by authorities, leaving one Secret Service agent and one would-be assassin dead. The second assassin was injured, but recovered. He was sentenced to death, but Harry Truman later commuted his sentence to life in prison. He was paroled thirty-four years following the incident.

In the wake of the assassination attempt, Congress enacted legislation that permanently authorized Secret Service protection of the president, his immediate family, the president-elect, and the vice-president, if requested. It was the event that created the modern Secret Service Agency.

———— A ————

Among my most enjoyable literary projects is a series of books I call *Homecoming Historicals*. Each of these books takes place in a modern-day high school, but the namesake of the school gets involved with the students in profound and creative ways. The first book in the series is the novel, *One Season of Hope*, featuring Harry Truman. In each of the books in the series, I have a recognized expert help with my research and write the Foreword to the book. Dennis Giangreco, who is an award-winning author and Truman historian, filled that role in *One Season of Hope.* Dennis helped me and my readers understand that Harry Truman was an ordinary man who became extraordinary because the time in which he lived and the situations he faced demanded it.

President Truman rallied the country and the free world together to win World War II. By word and deed, he taught us that everyone has a role in victory, and we can all succeed together if we focus on the common good.

27

"You can never quit. Winners never quit,
and quitters never win."

—TED TURNER

IT CAN NEVER BE SAID that Ted Turner is a quitter. His intellect, persistence, and insightful nature, have earned him a seat at the winner's table. His accomplishments are impressive and countless. The business tycoon and cable news pioneer began his career working for his father's billboard business, which he took over in 1963 after his father's death. Robert Edward "Ted" Turner III, an American entrepreneur, television producer, media mogul, and philanthropist, was born in Cincinnati, Ohio, on November 19, 1938.

At age 9, Ted Turner's family relocated to Savannah, Georgia. He attended a private boys' preparatory school in Chattanooga, Tennessee, Georgia Military Academy near Atlanta, and he attended Brown University. At Brown, he was vice president of the Brown Debating Union, competing in American and British Parliamentary Debate, and captain of the sailing team.

Ted Turner has built a media empire that began in 1970 with Turner Broadcasting System (TBS).

TBS pioneered Turner's "superstation" concept on cable television. He revolutionized the news media by developing the first 24-hour, news-only station, Cable News Network (CNN), and headline news, covering such events as the Space

Shuttle Challenger disaster in 1986 and the Persian Gulf War in 1991. With the purchase of the Atlanta Braves baseball team, he popularized the franchise in Georgia. In 1976, he acquired the majority share of the Atlanta Hawks basketball team, and he brought back enthusiasm for professional wrestling when he purchased World Championship Wrestling (WCW).

In 1986, Ted Turner created the Goodwill Games to unite countries and provide a way for athletes to compete in light of the 1980 Summer Olympic Games political issues and subsequent boycott. The first Goodwill Games were held in Moscow in 1986, with over 3,000 athletes competing in a multisport event from seventy-nine countries. The event was televised on TBS Superstation.

In 1949, Ted Turner developed an interest in sailing when his father gave him a Penguin sailing dinghy. Once he learned the basics of jibing and tacking, there was no stopping him. In 1977, he entered America's Cup race. Manning his outdated yacht, *Courageous*, in a string of contests, he strategically defeated his opponents with expertly bold tacking, winning the right to defend America's Cup against the world's contenders. With his veteran crew, both highly experienced and young, they won America's Cup.

Perhaps his most notable feat of sailing was in August 1979 when he entered the Fastnet Race, which required boats to sail 605 nautical miles from Plymouth, England, around Fastnet Rock near the coast of Ireland circling back to Plymouth. Along the course, a massive storm hit, and a mere 92 of the 302 boats that began the race were able to finish. Twenty-two lives were lost, and countless more injured. With all of the tenacity he possessed, for Ted Turner, it was a matter of win or die. As other competitors' boats flipped by the gale-force winds, he kept his vessel, the *Tenacious*, at full sail. Though conditions were treacherous, he refused to quit. Ted Turner, and the *Tenacious*, won one of the ocean's deadliest sailboat races in history.

Over the years, Ted Turner, through Turner Enterprises, has devoted much of his assets to environmental causes. Until 2011, he was the largest private landowner in the United States, and he commits much of his land for ranches to raise bison meat. He has accumulated the largest herd in the world.

— A —

After losing my sight, I was frustrated by my inability to enjoy movies and television. I had a vague idea of adding soundtracks to existing programming to describe the visual elements of the show for millions of blind and visually impaired people. Realizing that such a venture would be a monumental task, I started thinking about people who could help me make it a reality. The first name that came to mind was Ted Turner, as he had already proven himself as a media pioneer by launching CNN, TBS Superstation, and all of his other combined media ventures. Ted Turner responded to a brief one-page letter I mailed to him, and thereby he became my mentor and friend.

When you're around Ted Turner, you are struck by his excitement, energy, and tenacity. In his quote, *"You can never quit. Winners never quit, and quitters never win,"* he reminds us that success is the inevitable result if we will simply persevere.

28

"In times like these, it helps to recall that there have always been times like these."

—PAUL HARVEY

PAUL HARVEY AURANDT, born on September 4, 1918, was not only a radio broadcaster for ABC News Radio, he was a "personality." Known simply as Paul Harvey, his *News and Comment* program that aired weekday mornings and middays on the weekends and Saturdays was a listening must for as many as 24 million Americans. *Paul Harvey News* was produced on 1,200 radio stations, 400 American Forces Network stations, and published in 300 newspapers.

He was known for his iconic catchphrases and strategic pauses for emphasis. At the start of his programs, he would begin with, "Hello Americans, this is Paul Harvey. Stand by for *news!*"—emphasis on the word *news*. At the end of the broadcast, he concluded with "Paul Harvey...good *day!*" Or, "Paul Harvey...good *night!*" As he moved from one segment of the program to another, he informed his audience by simply saying, "Page two" and "Page three." The last story of his broadcast was traditionally humorous, and he introduced it with, "And now from the 'For-what-it's-worth' department."

As part of his newscasts during World War II and later broadcasted on his series on ABC Radio Networks, *The Rest of the Story* was presented as little-known or forgotten facts covering a variety of subjects, usually the name of a well-known person or celebrity. He held back that detail in each program until the end of the story. In his conclusion, he wrapped up the program with his legendary tag line and pause, "And now you know...the *rest* of the story."

From the series' inception, the scripts were created and written by his son, Paul Harvey Jr., who also acted as substitute host in his father's absence. Paul Harvey's stories were published in 1977 by his son in book form—*The Rest of the Story*, followed by *More of Paul Harvey's The Rest of the Story*.

Paul Harvey was more than a radio personality. He was an avid pilot and briefly served in the U.S. Army Air Corps. A member of several aircraft associations, including Aircraft Owners and Pilots Association (AOPA) and Experimental Aircraft Association (EAA), he was also an early investor in the aircraft manufacturing company Cirrus Aircraft, which is based in Duluth, Minnesota. Founded in 1984, the company produces several versions of its three certificated single-engine light aircraft models manufactured out of composite materials.

According to contributing editor, Barry Schiff of the *AOPA Pilot Magazine*, Paul Harvey coined the term "skyjack," and he made the terms "Reaganomics" and "guesstimate" popular. His career expanded from 1951 to 2008. On February 28, 2009, Paul Harvey died at the age of 90 in Phoenix, Arizona. As his son eulogized, "Millions have lost a friend."

Paul Harvey was elected to the National Association of Broadcasters National Radio Hall of Fame and the Oklahoma Hall of Fame. He also appeared on the Gallup Poll list of America's most admired men. In 2005, he was awarded the Presidential Medal of Freedom by President George W. Bush, the United States most prestigious civilian award. Upon presenting the award, President Bush summarized Paul Harvey's career, saying, "He first went on the air in 1933, and he's been heard nationwide for fifty-four years. Americans like the sound of his voice…over the decades we have come to recognize in that voice some of the finest qualities of our country: patriotism, the good humor, the kindness, and common sense of Americans."

Among the most humbling experiences in my life was being inducted into the Oklahoma Hall of Fame. This honor put me in the company of fellow Oklahomans such as Will Rogers, Mickey Mantle, and Paul Harvey. As a young child in either my parents' or grandparents' homes, I remember everyone gathering around and turning up the radio to hear the morning and noon broadcasts of *Paul Harvey's News and Comment*. These broadcasts were available to virtually every American and millions of people worldwide via Armed Forces Radio.

Paul Harvey had more influence with a larger group of people than anyone has on the scene today. Among the many things I appreciated about Paul Harvey was his ability to give the news factually, and then share his opinion via his commentary while keeping the two elements separated.

In his quote, *"In times like these, it helps to recall that there have always been times like these,"* Paul Harvey echoes the sentiment that there's nothing new under the sun. History can teach us many lessons, and it's comforting to remember that whatever we may be facing, our ancestors likely faced something similar in the past.

29

*"If I knew I was going to live this long,
I'd have taken better care of myself."*

—MICKEY MANTLE

BORN ON OCTOBER 20, 1932, in Spavinaw, Oklahoma, Mickey Charles Mantle, nicknamed "The Commerce Comet" and "The Mick," was named by his baseball-loving father in honor of Detroit Tiger catcher Mickey Cochrane, who, in 1947, was inducted into the Baseball Hall of Fame.

Considered one of the game's best sluggers and most outstanding players in Major League Baseball, Mickey Mantle maintained an impressive career playing with the New York Yankees from 1951 to 1968. He is also considered the greatest switch hitter of all time and is the only player in history to hit 150 home runs from both sides of the plate. In 1960, he hit a ball, left-handed, that cleared the right-field roof of Detroit's Tiger Stadium. It was estimated by historian Mark Gallagher to have traveled 643 feet.

Mantle was an all-around athlete in high school. Although baseball was his first passion, he also played basketball and football. A scout recognized his talent in football, and he was offered a football scholarship to the University of Oklahoma. As a sophomore, his sports career was nearly ended when he was kicked on the left shin during a practice game and developed the crippling disease, osteomyelitis, in his left ankle. Treated at the children's hospital in Oklahoma City, Oklahoma, the newly developed drug, penicillin, saved his leg from amputation.

Mickey Mantle learned to switch-hit at an early age by hitting pitches against his father, Elvin Charles "Mutt" Mantle, and his grandfather, George Mantle. Practicing with his father, he batted left-handed to his father's right-handed pitches, and he batted right-handed when his grandfather pitched to him with his left hand.

At age 19, a New York Yankees scout saw him play on his high school team and signed him to the minor league for two years before joining the major league team. He was promoted to the majors as a right fielder in 1951. Major league catcher and manager Bill Dickey once recalled of Mickey Mantle, "He's the greatest prospect I've seen in my time, and I go back quite a ways. I'll swear I expect to see that boy just take off and fly any time."

With an impressive record, among his many accomplishments are his all-time World Series records for having hit 18 home runs, 42 runs scored, and 40 RBIs (runs batted in).

Mickey Mantle wanted to be remembered as a stellar teammate. Fellow Yankees player, Joe Collins, recalled that "Mickey was the type of guy who cared about you as a person. As a teammate, he never complained about his injuries and always tried to lead by example. He always had that country boy attitude that made you feel at ease. He was a huge star, but he never treated you like he was better than you."

In 1964, Mickey Mantle was inducted into the Oklahoma Hall of Fame; in 1969 he received the Gold Plate Award of the American Academy of Achievement; in 1974, his first year of eligibility, he was elected to the Baseball Hall of Fame; and in 1999 he was elected into the Major League Baseball All-Century Team. A year after his death, Mantle's Monument Park plaque was replaced with a monument. On it were the words, "A great teammate—a magnificent Yankee who left a legacy of unequaled courage."

On August 13, 1995, Mickey Mantle died. The New York Yankees played the Cleveland Indians that day, and he was honored with a tribute. The team wore black mourning bands topped by the #7 on their left sleeves for the remainder of the season.

At his funeral, organist Eddie Layton played "Somewhere Over the Rainbow" because Mickey Mantle had once told him it was his favorite song. Roy Clark played and sang, "Yesterday, When I Was Young." In eulogizing him, sportscaster Bob Costas described him as "a fragile hero to whom we had an emotional attachment so strong and lasting that it defied logic." He continued, "In the last year of his life, Mickey Mantle, always so hard on himself, finally came to accept and appreciate the distinction between a role model and a hero. The first, he often was not. The second, he always will be. And, in the end, people got it."

At Mickey Mantle's request, second baseman, Bobby Richardson, obliged in reading the poem, *God's Hall of Fame*, at his funeral. It was the same poem Richardson recited for Roger Maris when he died.

In 1997, the Topps Baseball Card Company retired card number seven in his baseball flagship set in tribute to Mickey Mantle. His cards are highly popular and valuable among baseball card collectors—his 1952 card was sold in January 2021 for $5.2 million.

My father was a Minor League Baseball player, and his claim to fame was playing in a game against Mickey Mantle. That game marked a tale of two players in that by the next year, my father had a "real job" and never played competitive baseball again; and Mickey Mantle—as a 19-year-old—took his place in center field for the New York Yankees, filling the shoes of Babe Ruth and Joe DiMaggio as the Yankees' previous center fielders. In spite of injuries and setbacks, Mickey Mantle enjoyed a legendary career; and in his retirement, his struggles with alcoholism were made public and served to inspire many people dealing with their own addictions.

Mickey Mantle's quote, *"If I knew I was going to live this long, I'd have taken better care of myself,"* reminds us all that we are writing our own obituaries as we live our lives one day at a time. It's important to live our lives today in a way that will help us live the lives we want to live in the future.

30

"If you don't have time to do it right,
when will you have time to do it over?"

—JOHN WOODEN

NICKNAMED THE "WIZARD OF WESTWOOD," a moniker that he never took to, Coach John Robert Wooden was the "Greatest Coach of All Time," according to *The Sporting News* magazine. In a 2009 publication, the magazine listed the top fifty coaches in American history. The panel chose Coach Wooden as number one, receiving fifty-seven votes.

Coach Wooden and his wife, Nell Riley, wanted to stay in the Midwest and hoped to receive a coaching position with the University of Minnesota. Due to inclement weather, the call never came, so Coach Wooden accepted an offer from his second-team choice, the University of California, Los Angeles (UCLA). One day after he accepted the offer from UCLA, he received the call he had been waiting for from the University of Minnesota. However, he kept his commitment to UCLA Bruins, and the rest is history.

As head coach of the division one men's college basketball team, he won ten NCAA championships, seven consecutive NCAA championships, thirty-eight consecutive NCAA tournament victories, and four undefeated seasons. He won ten national championships, including seven in a row, in the last twelve years as head coach. John Wooden ended his coaching career at UCLA with a 620–147 record, winning .808 percent of his games—not to mention his two-year record at Indiana State University before taking the job at UCLA. After retiring from coaching, UCLA continued to honor Coach Wooden by giving him the title of Head Men's Basketball Coach Emeritus.

On November 17, 2006, Coach Wooden was honored for his contribution to college basketball as a member of the founding class of the National Collegiate Basketball Hall of Fame. He was further honored with the nation's highest civilian award, the Presidential Medal of Honor. It was presented to him on July 23, 2003, by President George W. Bush.

John Wooden is legendary for his forty-two years of teaching and coaching college basketball. But after he retired from basketball, he became one of America's leading authors, life coaches, and public speakers. He studied the teachings of Confucius, Aristotle, William Shakespeare, Abraham Lincoln, and many more, and he spent a lifetime documenting, collaborating, and sharing wisdom "The Wooden Way." John Wooden lectured and coauthored his book, *Coach Wooden's Pyramid of Success*, based on his method of victory. It reveals the philosophical building blocks for succeeding in basketball and life. In his later years, he was hired by corporations to deliver inspirational lectures.

When he was a freshman in high school, he met his future wife, Nell Riley. He was devoted to her throughout their fifty-three years of marriage, and the couple had two children. Nell lost her battle with breast cancer and died on March 21, 1985. He honored her memory by visiting her crypt at the mausoleum on the 21st day of each month. When he returned home, he wrote her a love letter, placed it in an envelope, and added it to the collection over the years. He kept them on her pillow. In the last months of his life, John Wooden's eyesight failed, and the letters stopped.

CHAPTER 30

After her death, John Wooden relied on his faith to see him through her loss, saying,

> I have always tried to make it clear that basketball
> is not the ultimate. It is of small importance in
> comparison to the total life we live. There is only one
> kind of life that truly wins, and that is the one that
> places faith in the hands of the Savior. If I were ever
> prosecuted for my religion, I truly hope there would be
> enough evidence to convict me.

For the last twenty-five years of his life, after the passing of his wife, his daughter Nancy Wooden Muehlhausen spent much time with her father and served as his escort to events and outings. She remembered, "Maybe the greatest lesson he taught me was the importance of always being gracious because you never know who you have a chance to influence."

John Wooden died on June 4, 2010, at 99. In his final days, he knew he was dying. He asked that he get a good shave, for he wanted to look his best when he saw his bride in heaven. In the end, it can be said that John Wooden did everything right.

Many years ago, I stopped calculating my net worth or wealth based upon how much money I had; instead, I began making the calculation based on the quality of my friends. I can honestly say that I am a wealthier man because Coach John Wooden was my friend.

I remember each March, during my grade school years, my father and I would watch the NCAA college basketball tournament. We enjoyed rooting for the UCLA Bruins, and it seemed like a foregone conclusion each year that they would be in the tournament, go to the finals, and play for the championship.

Unlike most coaches, John Wooden calmly sat at the end of the bench holding his rolled up program and studiously observed the game. While other coaches yelled, turned red in the face, and threw things, Coach Wooden modeled the poise and self-control that he demanded of his players. He thought of himself more as a teacher than a coach. He felt his subject was life, and a basketball court was his classroom.

I will never forget the day when he called our office and requested several autographed books for some of his former players, including Kareen Abdul Jabbar and Bill Walton. He and I spoke that day, and it began a dialogue that lasted almost five years until he passed away a few months short of his 100th birthday.

In his quote, *"If you don't have time to do it right, when will you have time to do it over,"* Coach John Wooden reminds us all that there is a right way and a wrong way to do everything.

31

*"I've made my share of mistakes along the way,
but if I have changed even one life for the better,
I haven't lived in vain."*

—MUHAMMAD ALI

CASSIUS MARCELLUS CLAY JR. was born on January 17, 1942, in Louisville, Kentucky. Named for his father, he was renamed Muhammad Ali by the Nation of Islam in 1964. Frequently, he referred to himself as "The Greatest," and many people agreed. Notably, the 6'3" athlete had been ranked the "Greatest Heavyweight Boxer of All Time" and the "Greatest Sportsman of the 20th Century" by *Sports Illustrated.* The BBC named him "Sports Personality of the Century." It was not surprising that the name Muhammad, meaning "one who is worthy of praise," and Ali, connoting "most high," was given to him.

Ali fought sixty-one professional career fights, winning fifty-six and declaring only five losses. He won thirty-seven of his bouts by knockout.

Few journalists at the time recognized him as Muhammad Ali. To them, he was Cassius Clay. Howard Cosell was the exception. The two men formed an unlikely friendship that lasted over thirty years. Howard Cosell was a pompous commentator, and Muhammad Ali was a brash and arrogant personality that fans idolized. Together, they brought excitement to the sport of boxing.

At 12 years old, Ali's interest in boxing was sparked by Louisville policeman Joe Martin, who happened upon him. The boy was furious over the theft of his bicycle, and he told the policeman he was going to "whup" the guy who stole it. Officer Martin told the then Cassius Clay that he had better learn to box first. At the time, Ali did not give the advice a second thought until one day he saw an amateur boxing match on the local television program, *Tomorrow's Champions*, and that changed his life.

In 1954, Muhammad Ali made his amateur boxing debut against Ronnie O'Keefe, winning by split decision. He went on to win six "Kentucky Golden Gloves" titles, two national "Golden Gloves" titles, an "Amateur Athletic Union" national title, and the light-heavyweight gold medal in the 1960 Summer Olympics in Rome. His amateur record boasted 100 wins and 5 losses.

When he was 18, he made his professional debut. He won a six-round decision over Tunney Morgan Hunsaker, a professional boxer who served as police chief of Fayetteville, West Virginia. This win set him in the direction of a heavyweight champion, who won the title three times in his twenty-one-year career.

The charismatic Muhammad Ali had a unique way of entertaining his fans, at the same time taunting his challengers. With his smooth, rhythmic tone, coupled with his creative freestyle poetry, he flashed his bulky ego and comically intimidated his opponents with trash-talking.

Confident and colorful, he told the press, "I've done something new for this fight. I've wrestled with alligators. I've tussled with a whale. I done handcuffed lightning and thrown thunder in jail. You know I'm bad. Just last week, I murdered a rock...injured a stone...hospitalized a brick. I'm so mean, I make medicine sick." His most notable poem was delivered before his fight with George Foreman, saying, "I float like a butterfly, sting like a bee. His hands can't hit what his eyes can't see. Now you see me, now you don't. George thinks he will, but I know he won't."

From his poetry style, some consider Muhammad Ali to be the first musical rapper. In 1963, he released an album titled *I am the Greatest* in his iconic spoken-word music on the Columbia Records label; and a year later, he recorded a cover version of the rhythm and blues song, *Stand by Me*, which sold 500,000 copies. It reached number sixty-one on the album chart and was nominated for a Grammy Award. His second Grammy nomination came for "Best Recording for Children" in 1976 with his novelty record, *The Adventures of Ali and His Gang vs. Mr. Tooth Decay*.

Muhammad Ali was a world-class boxer and an activist who stood for peace and became well-known for his stand as a conscientious objector to the Vietnam War. He was a philanthropist who devoted his life to helping others. He wanted all people to be happy.

Father of nine children, his daughter Hana wrote of him, "His love for people was extraordinary. I would get home from school to find homeless families sleeping in our guest room. He'd see them on the street, pile them into his Rolls Royce and bring them home. He'd buy them clothes, take them to hotels, and pay the bills for months in advance."

In Los Angeles on January 19, 1981, Muhammad Ali talked a suicidal man down from jumping off a ninth-floor ledge. The event made national news.

Life as a boxer took its toll on Muhammad Ali. In 1984, though he remained active, he was diagnosed with Parkinson's disease, which can sometimes result from head trauma or violent physical activity. He began working in 1998 with actor Michael J. Fox, who also suffers from Parkinson's disease, and the Fox Foundation for Parkinson's Disease to raise awareness and seek funding for research to find a cure. Together, they made a joint appearance before Congress for support.

Muhammad Ali was presented with the Presidential Citizens Medal on January 8, 2001, by President Bill Clinton. In November 2005, he received the Presidential Medal of Freedom presented by President George W. Bush.

On June 3, 2016, Muhammad Ali died of respiratory illness at age 74. Throughout his life, he proved that even a young man who had difficulties reading and writing in school and who was diagnosed with dyslexia could change lives and be "Great."

———— A ————

In our offices and studios, we have photos, memorabilia, and awards from more than thirty years in the movie, book, and television industry. Periodically, we have groups of people visit our facilities to take a tour and look at the signed photos, movie posters, presidential letters, awards, and sports memorabilia. Out of everything we have, people seem to be most impressed and excited about a boxing glove signed by Muhammad Ali.

As a young man, Muhammad Ali declared to the world that he was "the Greatest of all Time." Over the next several decades, he set out to prove it. Ali became much more than an Olympic gold medalist or the Heavy Weight Champion of the World. He became a worldwide icon who transcended sports.

In his quote, *"I've made my share of mistakes along the way, but if I have changed even one life for the better, I haven't lived in vain,"* Muhammad Ali gives us a perspective that reminds us all that whatever the issue at hand or the factors involved, in the final analysis, it's not about us.

32

"Success depends almost entirely on how effectively you learn to manage the game's two ultimate adversaries: the course and yourself."

—JACK NICKLAUS

JACK WILLIAM NICKLAUS, nicknamed "The Golden Bear," coined by Australian sportswriter Don Lawrence during the 1967 U.S. Open tournament for his blonde hair and burly physique, was born January 21, 1940. The retired professional golfer was raised in Columbus, Ohio, and is one of the greatest golfers of all time. He became a professional golfer at age 21 and had 164 major tournaments to his credit—more than any other player. In his over one-quarter of a century career, he won 117 professional tournaments and a record 18 major championships. He won the Masters tournament six times, four U.S. Open titles, three British Open titles, and five PGA Championship tournaments. He won 73 PGA Tour victories and various other global tournaments.

Teaming with his fierce competitors and great lifelong friends, Arnold Palmer and Gary Player, Nicklaus built an empire designing nearly 1,000 golf courses worldwide.

Jack Nicklaus overcame a mild case of polio when he was 13 years old. In 2015, he commented on the dreadful disease, saying,

Polio is just a memory now, but it was a horrible
disease. I contracted it when I was 13—a year or two
before Jonas Salk's polio vaccine was made available.
I started feeling stiff, my joints ached, and over a two-
week period, I lost my coordination and 20 pounds.
I recovered after a few weeks, but I still may suffer from
post-polio syndrome. My whole career, my joints have
gotten awfully sore at times.

In his youth, Jack Nicklaus found success in many sports,
including football, baseball, tennis, and track and field. He
enjoyed the game of golf when, at age 10, he scored a 51 for his
first nine holes of play ever.

In college, he majored in pre-pharmacy at Ohio State
University from 1957 to 1961, maintaining good grades in his
first three years. After graduation, he intended to follow in his
father's footsteps and become a pharmacist. However, as his golf
achievements grew, his career path changed, and he decided
to pursue his amateur golf career while earning a living selling
insurance.

Not long after becoming the first amateur golfer to win
the Masters, he announced he would turn professional to
support his new wife, Barbara, and their first of five children.
Subsequently, he fell short of credits to earn his college degree;
but in a goodwill gesture in 1972, Ohio State University granted
him an honorary doctorate.

Jack Nicklaus' last major title was in 1986. At age 46,
he became the oldest Master winner in history. He became a
member of the World Golf Hall of Fame in 1974, the PGA
named him Golfer of the Century in 1988, and he joined the
Senior Tour in 1990, winning the U.S. Senior Open in 1991
and 1993.

CHAPTER 32

In 2005, Jack Nicklaus retired from playing in professional tournaments.

———— A ————

My novels and nonfiction books have allowed me to meet some amazing people and create some tremendous friendships. After reading one of my books, Jack Nicklaus contacted me; and from that day forward, whenever a book of mine is released, a signed copy is sent to Jack and Barbara Nicklaus. Without fail, I receive a handwritten note of thanks and encouragement.

Jack Nicklaus set a standard that will likely never be matched in a sport that demands both mental and physical mastery. He is known for his mental toughness. Whenever I think of the word *tenacity*, I think of Jack Nicklaus. In his quote, *"Success depends almost entirely on how effectively you learn to manage the game's two ultimate adversaries: the course and yourself,"* he reveals the truth that, regardless of the endeavor, there is no victory over an obstacle or opponent until we are victorious in our own heart, mind, and soul.

If we want to control our destiny in the future, we have to control ourselves today.

33

*"I don't know what would have happened
to me if I hadn't been able to hear."*

—RAY CHARLES

RAY CHARLES ROBINSON JR., known professionally as Ray
Charles, was and is still admired as a singer, songwriter, pianist,
and composer with a career that spanned almost sixty years. Born
September 23, 1930, in Albany, Georgia, he is often referred
to as "the Genius" for pioneering the soul music genre during
the 1950s. He combined the sounds of blues, jazz, rhythm and
blues, and gospel styles into his music. He was known simply as
"Brother Ray" to his friends and fellow musicians.

There was deep love between Ray Charles and his mother.
Shortly after his birth, his single mother, Aretha, only 17 at the
time, moved to Florida, where she had lived before giving birth
to her first son. Until her death, Aretha took in washing and
ironing to survive, but the family lived in poverty despite her
efforts.

Aretha gave birth to a second son, George, who drowned
in his mother's washtub at the age of 4. Though Ray Charles
tried to save his brother, he could not be revived. Later in life,
Ray Charles recalled that George was a bright boy. "He could
have done great things," he said. In the cruelest of ironies, seeing
his brother drown would be one of the last things he would see
clearly.

At the age of 5, his vision became blurred. He remembered, "Faraway distances were fading. I was like a guy who stands on top of a mountain and one week sees fifteen miles off, the next week only ten miles, the third week only five. At first, I could still make out large forms, then only colors, then only night from day." Two years later, he was sightless. Though not certain, his condition is thought to have resulted from abnormally high fluid pressure in his eyes, known as glaucoma. Initially, he challenged his mother's decision to send him to the Florida School for the Deaf and the Blind in St. Augustine.

Ray Charles became interested in music at the age of 3 when he heard Wylie Pitman play "Boogie-woogie" on an old upright piano at Wylie Pitman's Red Wing Café, a combination grocery store, restaurant, and nightclub. It was there that Pitman taught Ray Charles to play the piano.

His musical talents advanced at school, where his teacher, Mrs. Lawrence, taught him to play the classical piano music of Bach, Mozart, and Beethoven. She also taught him how to read braille music. The process was challenging to pick up. It required learning the left-hand movements while reading braille with his right hand, and vice versa, learning the right-hand movements while reading the music with his left hand. Once that was mastered, he combined the two parts.

While away at school, Ray Charles' mother died in the spring of 1945. He was 14 years old, and her death came as a shock. First, he had felt the heartbreak of his brother George's tragic death; then, he faced the loss of his mother. Rather than returning to school, he set out to make a living. He had three rules: no dogs, no cane, and no guitar, for all symbolized blindness in his mind, and he did not want to be viewed that way.

By the early 1960s, Ray Charles was a successful music artist. He owned an airplane and was escorted by an entourage.

In his book, *The Great American Popular Singers*, published in 1974, writer and music critic Henry Pleasants stated that Ray Charles possessed one of the most recognized voices in American music. In the critic's words:

Sinatra, and Bing Crosby before him, had been masters of words. Ray Charles is a master of sounds. His records disclose an extraordinary assortment of slurs, glides, turns, shrieks, wails, breaks, shouts, screams, and hollers, all wonderfully controlled, disciplined by inspired musicianship, and harnessed to ingenious subtleties of harmony, dynamics, and rhythm... It is either the singing of a man whose vocabulary is inadequate to express what is in his heart and mind or of one whose feelings are too intense for satisfactory verbal or conventionally melodic articulation. He can't tell it to you. He can't even sing it to you. He has to cry out to you or shout to you, in tones eloquent of despair—or exaltation. The voice alone, with little assistance from the text or the notated music, conveys the message.

Throughout his life, Ray Charles found himself at the mercy of drug addiction. On his road to recovery, he began playing chess. As part of his therapy, his psychiatrist, Frederick Hacker, taught him to play. They met three times a week, and he used a special board with raised square holes for the chess pieces. In 2002, though he lost the match, he had the privilege of playing against the American grandmaster and former United States chess champion Larry Evans.

Throughout his career, he received many honors and distinctions. In 1987, he was honored with a Grammy Lifetime

Achievement Award, and ten of his recordings were inducted into the Grammy Hall of Fame. In 1979, Ray Charles' version of the song, "Georgia on My Mind," composed by Hoagy Carmichael, with lyrics by Stuart Gorrell, became the State song of Georgia.

Ray Charles once said, "I don't know what would have happened to me if I hadn't been able to hear." The sounds of music were his life. Ironically, he founded The Robinson Foundation for Hearing Disorders, specifically to provide financial contributions to institutions involved in research and education relating to hearing loss and disorders. In 2006, it was renamed the "Ray Charles Foundation."

On June 10, 2004, at the age of 73, Ray Charles died at his home in Beverly Hills, California, of complications resulting from liver failure. Two months after his death, his final album, *Genius Loves Company*, featuring duets by numerous recording artists, was released. At his memorial service, his favorite song, "Over the Rainbow," from the album in which he sang in duet with Johnny Mathis, was played.

Ray Charles won countless accolades, awards, and distinctions, in his lifetime, including his star on the Hollywood Walk of Fame. In the Ray Charles Plaza in Albany, Georgia, stands a statue in his likeness sitting at a grand piano.

—— A ——

I met Ray Charles at a critical point in my life, and we seemed to cross paths at important junctures in my career right up until his passing. As a young man, my greatest ambition was to be a professional football player. During a routine physical before the beginning of another season, I was diagnosed with a condition that would cause me to lose my sight. Since I could still see well enough to get around on my own at that point, I decided to go to the state fair and try to forget about my troubles and the fateful diagnosis.

There was a huge banner on the arena that said, "Free concert." I didn't know who was playing or when it started, but "free" really fit my budget. So I wondered in and sat in the front row. I was lost in thoughts of fear and anxiety about becoming blind, so I really didn't notice that the arena had filled up around me until a voice I will never forget echoed throughout the arena, "Ladies and gentlemen, please welcome to the state fair, the one, the only, the legend, Ray Charles!"

Ray was mesmerizing, and I realized that if a dream is big enough, even blindness couldn't extinguish it. Ten years later, I had reached a degree of success and was speaking at an international business conference in Madison Square Garden in New York. The promoter of that event had booked Ray Charles to play Carnegie Hall the following night, so I had an opportunity to go backstage and meet him. That meeting was the beginning of one of the most powerful connections in my life.

Ray's quote, *"I don't know what would have happened to me if I hadn't been able to hear,"* reminds us that we have to value what we have instead of lamenting the things we don't have.

34

*"Just because a man lacks the use of his eyes
doesn't mean he lacks vision."*

—STEVIE WONDER

KNOWN PROFESSIONALLY AS STEVIE WONDER, he was born Stevland Hardaway Judkins, on May 13, 1950, in Saginaw, Michigan, and became a talented singer, songwriter, musician, record producer, and multi-instrumental musician. He inspires others and has been labeled as a "musical genius." Stevie Wonder is one of the world's best-selling artists, and he has sold more than 100 million records throughout his career. He has championed humanitarian causes through his fame, such as AIDS awareness, drug use, and discrimination.

Earning a reputation as a one-person band, he redefined the conventions of rhythm and blues with his electronic musical instruments and synthesizers to give his music unique sounds and complex compositions.

Born six weeks early, Stevie Wonder soon developed an eye condition called retinopathy of prematurity. It is an eye disorder wherein the retinas detach. His condition was exacerbated by receiving too much oxygen in the incubator. It led to his losing all sight. This unfortunate circumstance did not hinder his success.

At age 4, his parents divorced, and his mother, Lula Mae Hardaway, moved to Detroit with her three children. There,

Stevie Wonder sang and played the harmonica in the church choir. His talents led him to sign with Motown's Tamla label at age 11. He was considered a child prodigy, which inspired his youthful stage name "Little Stevie Wonder."

Stevie Wonder attended Fitzgerald Elementary School, but after his first album, *The Jazz Soul of Little Stevie*, was released in 1962, he enrolled in the Michigan School for the Blind.

In 1963, his number one hit single, "Fingertips" hit the *Billboard Hot 100*, making the 13-year-old the youngest artist ever to top the chart. The musical number showcased his vocal talents and his instrumental gifts playing the bongos and the harmonica. In 2015, at age 65, Stevie Wonder delighted the audience when he recreated the vocal sound of "Little Stevie Wonder." Singing his first hit "Fingertips," live on the *Late Show with David Letterman*, he used what he called his "magic microphone" to transform his adult voice into his 12-year-old sound.

Tragically, on August 6, 1973, Stevie Wonder was involved in a severe automobile accident that left him in a coma for four days. On tour in Durham, North Carolina, to promote his new album, *Innervisions*, the car he was in, driven by his cousin John Wesley Harris, hit the back of a flatbed logging truck. While hospitalized, he received a visit from gospel singer Ira Tucker, who serenaded him with his song, "Higher Ground." It was reported that Stevie Wonder began moving his fingers in time with the keyboard movements of the song and slowly came out of his coma.

As a result of the crash, he temporarily lost his sense of smell, and the impact left a scar on his forehead. When suggested that he undergo plastic surgery to remove the mark, he declined, saying, "I will leave it as one of the scars of life I went through."

Stevie Wonder has won numerous awards, both musical and civil. He has won twenty-two Grammy Awards and received the coveted Lifetime Grammy Award in 1996. He won the Academy Award for Best Original Song for the 1984 film *The Woman in Red*. He is the first Motown artist and the second African-American musician to have won the award. Stevie Wonder has been inducted into the Rhythm and Blues Music Hall of Fame, Rock and Roll Hall of Fame, and has received a star on the Hollywood Walk of Fame. In 2021, he was the founding inductee of the Black Music and Entertainment Walk of Fame.

In 2014, Stevie Wonder was honored by President Barack Obama with the Presidential Medal of Freedom.

He is a musical genius whose life is an inspiration to others.

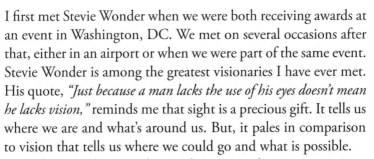

I first met Stevie Wonder when we were both receiving awards at an event in Washington, DC. We met on several occasions after that, either in an airport or when we were part of the same event. Stevie Wonder is among the greatest visionaries I have ever met. His quote, *"Just because a man lacks the use of his eyes doesn't mean he lacks vision,"* reminds me that sight is a precious gift. It tells us where we are and what's around us. But, it pales in comparison to vision that tells us where we could go and what is possible.

Whenever I'm struggling with my attitude or my optimism, Stevie Wonder's music can lift my spirits and clarify my vision. One of the most powerful forces in our lives is the vision we have of ourselves and the vision we hold of our future.

35

"If you possess something but you can't give it away,
then you don't possess it—it possesses you."

—FRANK SINATRA

WITH POPULAR SONGS such as "In the Wee Small Hours," "Come Fly with Me," "Only the Lonely," "Nice 'n' Easy," "New York, New York," and his trademark song, "My Way," Ol' Blue Eyes, referred to for his deep blue eyes, he is Frank Sinatra. He has sold an estimated 150 million records worldwide. From humble beginnings in Hoboken, New Jersey, the smooth, mellow sounds of Bing Crosby and the driving beat of big bands led by Harry James and Tommy Dorsey highly influenced Frank Sinatra's style and crooning persona. He made the young ladies squeal and scream, and couples romantically sway to his music.

Francis Albert Sinatra, born December 12, 1915, released his debut album, *The Voice of Frank Sinatra*, in 1946, and by the early 1950s, he became one of the best-known performers in Las Vegas as part of the "Rat Pack."

The "Rat Pack," originally referred to as the "Clan," consisted of A-lister friends in show business—singers, actors, and celebrity personalities—who met regularly to party at the home of Humphrey Bogart and Lauren Bacall in Los Angeles. Lauren Bacall nicknamed the group "Rat Pack" when she commented that the group looked like a rat pack. The name stuck. After Humphrey Bogart died in 1957, the group dwindled, and Frank

CHAPTER 35

Sinatra, Dean Martin, and Sammy Davis Jr. became the group's core members.

In the 1960s, the name "Rat Pack" was publicly and forever identified with Frank Sinatra, Dean Martin, Sammy Davis Jr., Joey Bishop, and Peter Lawford, brother-in-law to John F. Kennedy. Unfortunately, after a disagreement with Frank Sinatra in 1962, Peter Lawford was excluded from the group. Together, they performed in Las Vegas casinos, entertaining audiences with their song, dance, and light-hearted comedic antics. Together, the "Rat Pack" appeared in the films *Ocean's 11*, *Sergeants 3*, *Four for Texas*, and *Robin and the 7 Hoods*, with Bing Crosby substituting for Peter Lawford.

Frank Sinatra already had a successful film career before performing with the "Rat Pack." He won an Academy Award for his role in *From Here to Eternity*. He also starred in *The Man with the Golden Arm*, *The Manchurian Candidate*, *On the Town*, *Guys and Dolls*, *High Society*, and *Pal Joey*, to name a few. Frank Sinatra also found success in television with *The Frank Sinatra Show*. At that time, he performed with the "Rat Pack," and Frank Sinatra hit number one on the *Billboard* charts with his song, "Strangers in the Night," which won him a Grammy for record of the year.

Frank Sinatra died on May 14, 1998. The words "The Best is Yet to Come" and "Beloved Husband and Father" are imprinted on his grave marker.

The day after his death, the lights on the Empire State Building in New York City, New York, were lit up in the color blue, and the lights of the Las Vegas Strip, where he performed throughout his career, were dimmed in his honor. For one minute, all casinos ceased gambling. Throughout that month, there was a substantial increase in record sales worldwide, according to *Billboard*.

Frank Sinatra has been considered the most significant American male pop singer of the 20th century. It is not surprising that his songs and his easy, romantic sound are still heard worldwide. Music history remembers him for his unique combination of voice and showmanship. The legend from Hoboken, New Jersey, still inspires the music industry, and a little romance too.

I had the privilege of interviewing Frank Sinatra during the early days of our company, the Narrative Television Network. Getting an interview with Mr. Sinatra did a great deal to enhance our notoriety and reputation. He was the embodiment of the overused adage, "larger than life." Frank Sinatra's generosity became legendary throughout the entertainment industry. He was known to buy cars, pay off homes, or cover outstanding medical bills for people in need, whether he really knew them or not. He was generous with his time and talent, which was apparent by the fact that he was willing to do an interview with me at a point when our Narrative Television Network was brand-new and struggling to get a foothold in the business.

One of my enduring memories occurred after I completed my interview with Mr. Sinatra, and I was walking with our production crew toward the elevators. He called out to me in that legendary Frank Sinatra voice, "Hey kid, I hope you live to be a hundred years old and the last thing you ever hear is me singing you a song."

36

"Life is hard. After all, it kills you."

—KATHARINE HEPBURN

KATHARINE HOUGHTON HEPBURN was a Hollywood leading lady who enjoyed a career that spanned sixty-six years. She appeared in forty-four feature films, eight television movies, and thirty-three Broadway and theatre productions. On-screen and off, she was outspoken, headstrong, assertive, yet sophisticated, and her performances ranged from dramatic roles to screwball comedies. Although she was American, she spoke in a Mid-Atlantic or Transatlantic accent, much like Cary Grant, with clarity of diction.

The second of six children, she was born on May 12, 1907, in Hartford, Connecticut, to an extraordinarily wealthy, highly-educated family, whose parents she described as "fascinating" and who "gave her freedom from fear." Attending the all-women Bryn Mawr College in Pennsylvania, like her mother before her, she graduated with a degree in history and philosophy in 1928.

Her father, Thomas Hepburn, was a urologist. He was a founder of the New England Social Hygiene Association, which was established to educate the public about socially transmitted diseases. Her mother, Katharine Martha Houghton Hepburn, was a social activist and supported women's rights. She was also the granddaughter of Amory Houghton, who founded the Corning Glass Works, a multinational technology company that specializes in glass, ceramics, and related materials, in 1851. It remains viable today.

Katharine Hepburn was well known for her strength, individualism, independence, spirited personality, and tomboy fashion style. These traits sometimes got her into trouble and caused her to lose roles for which she was hired. In 1990, she was recognized for her lifetime accomplishments in the arts with the Kennedy Center Honors Tribute hosted by Angela Lansbury, Glenn Close, and Lauren Bacall. In the tribute, Angela Lansbury recalled her eccentricity, saying that "Kate," as she was commonly called, "Was told by the heads of RKO that no self-respecting actress would ever wear dungarees in public. She told them she agreed completely, stripped them off, and strolled through the lot in her undergarments. She wore trousers and refused to coo like a starlet. They called her 'Katharine of Arrogance.'"

She made her theatre debut in 1928, gained Hollywood success in 1932, and made her final screen appearance in 1994 at age 87.

Throughout her career, Katharine Hepburn won four Academy Awards for Best Actress, four Oscars—three of the Oscars awarded after age 60—and an Emmy Award. In 1999, the American Film Institute named her the most outstanding female star of classic Hollywood cinema. She received a Lifetime Achievement Award from the Screen Actors Guild in 1979.

In the 1940 film, *The Philadelphia Story*, alongside Cary Grant and Jimmy Stewart, she played her most cherished role as a society brat brought down to earth by love. In her role in the *Woman of the Year* in 1942, she met Spencer Tracy for the first time, and they began a lifelong on-screen and off-screen affection for each other. The first day on the set, it was said that Katharine Hepburn told Spencer Tracy, "I'm afraid I'm too tall for you." Though a mere two inches taller, he replied, "Don't worry, Miss Hepburn, I'll soon cut you down to my size." They paired together in nine movies, remaining close until he died in 1967.

Katharine Hepburn was known for her gender-bending style, defying all sense of fashion for women of her era. She wore trousers rather than skirts at a time in history when women did not dare. In her words, "The thing that drove me out of skirts was the stocking situation…that's why I've always worn pants. That way, you can always go barefoot." Katharine Hepburn influenced the fashion world and pioneered the stylish look for women. Costume designer Edith Head once said, "One does not design for Miss Hepburn. One designs with her. She's a real professional, and she has very definite feelings about what things are right for her, whether it has to do with costumes, scripts, or her entire lifestyle." Today, a mere search will produce numerous websites featuring the branded "Katharine Hepburn trousers."

In her 1979 film, *The Corn Is Green*, critics noticed that she had a "palsy that kept her head trembling." First thought to be Parkinson's disease, it was discovered that she suffered from a condition called Essential Tremors, which she inherited from her grandfather. The medical condition caused her head to quiver and her hands to tremble.

Katharine Hepburn died on June 29, 2003, at age 96. Though she is gone, she will be remembered through the entertaining films she left behind.

There are certain people who are in the right place at the right time so that their lives intersect with ours. For me, Katharine Hepburn will always be remembered as one of those people who impacted my life personally and professionally as our paths crossed.

When I began my company, the Narrative Television Network, we contracted to provide hundreds of broadcast stations and cable systems with two-hour blocks of programming which we made accessible for blind and visually impaired people. We had added a number of our description soundtracks to classic movies, and I felt we were ready to launch our network when it was brought to my attention that our movies averaged only an hour and a half in length, so we were a half-hour short in our delivery to our affiliates.

The only solution I could devise involved me hosting a talk show to interview the stars from our films. We sent out hundreds of letters, but the first and most significant response came from Katharine Hepburn. Once I booked Katharine Hepburn on our show, it seemed like everyone in Hollywood wanted to do an interview with me. I expressed my gratitude by saying, "Thank you doesn't seem like enough for what you have done for us and the special people we serve." As was her custom, her response was short and simple, *"Thank you is always enough. It's really all we have."*

37

"Someone's sitting in the shade today because someone planted a tree a long time ago."

—WARREN BUFFETT

FROM AN EARLY AGE, Warren Edward Buffett showed boundless aptitude in money, investments, and the stock market. The second of three children, he was born in Omaha, Nebraska, on August 30, 1930, where he continues to reside. His father, Howard Homan Buffett, a stockbroker who turned to politics and was a four-term United States Representative for Nebraska, largely influenced him. Warren Buffett became an essential and influential person in the financial market, a highly successful investor, and philanthropist concerned with healthcare reform, economic and human wellness, and curbing population growth. He is currently the chairman and CEO of Berkshire Hathaway, a multinational conglomerate holding company that originated as a textile manufacturing company in 1806.

Upon graduating from Woodrow Wilson High School in 1947, Warren Buffett was tagged in his senior yearbook photo with the words, "likes math; a future stockbroker." At age 7, Warren Buffett was inspired by a book he borrowed from the Omaha Public Library titled, *One Thousand Ways to Make $1,000*, which set the stage for his future.

As a young man, Buffett spent time in the customers' lounge of a regional stock brokerage firm near his father's office.

Intrigued with the world's largest stock market, Warren Buffett visited the New York Stock Exchange. He was 10 years old. He made his first investment at age 11, when he bought three shares of Cities Service Preferred, at $38 per share, for himself, and three for his older sister, Doris. Initially, the stock rapidly declined to only $27 per share, but Warren Buffett held on until the price reached $40 then sold it for a small profit. He would have made considerably more when the price shot up to nearly $200 per share had he held it.

Warren Buffett was a youthful entrepreneur. He earned money working various jobs, including selling chewing gum, Coca-Cola bottles, and weekly magazines door-to-door. He worked in his grandfather's grocery store, delivered newspapers, sold golf balls and stamps, and detailed cars. As a sophomore in high school, Warren Buffett and a friend purchased a used pinball machine for $25. He placed it in the town's barbershop, and within months they had enough money to buy several more. One year later, they sold the business for $1,200.

In high school, Buffett invested his earnings in real estate. He purchased land when he was 14 years old with $1,200 from his savings. At 15, he delivered *Washington Post* newspapers and invested his earnings in his father's business. With his profits, he bought a forty-acre farm worked by a tenant farmer.

Warren Buffett graduated from the University of Nebraska at age 19. He enrolled in Columbia Business School and developed his investment philosophy with the help of value investing pioneer Benjamin Graham before attending the New York Institute of Finance. By the time he graduated, he had accumulated $9,800 in savings, a significant sum in 1949.

In 1956, he created Buffett Partnership, Ltd, with $100. He took on seven partners, including his sister, Doris, his Aunt Alice, and his father-in-law, and he continued to partner with other investors. A group led by Warren Buffett bought Berkshire Hathaway at a reasonable price in 1965 and created a diversified holding company. The organization now owns numerous top-brand companies.

Warren Buffett became a millionaire at age 33 and a billionaire at 55. Though he has acquired wealth in the billions of dollars, he remains personally frugal and donates significant amounts to worthy causes. Father of three, his children will not inherit a large portion of his wealth. In his words, he stated, "I want to give my kids just enough so that they would feel that they could do anything, but not so much that they would feel like doing nothing."

Warren Buffett has been one of the most influential people in America. He is a sought-after advisor to individuals and governments. When asked advice about buying stocks, he said, "Initial public offerings (IPO) of stock are almost always bad investments. Investors should be looking to companies that will have good value in ten years." With his business savvy and massive success, Warren Buffett has been dubbed the "Oracle" or "Sage" of Omaha.

—— A ——

There are a handful of people in the world who are significantly better than most everyone in their chosen field. For more than half a century, Warren Buffett's investment results have baffled experts and outpaced most other investment professionals. I remember the day I held my breath and paid a six-figure price to buy one share of Warren Buffett's company Berkshire Hathaway. This gave me the right to go to his annual meetings and receive his investment updates. The education I received from Warren Buffett was priceless, and my investment has more than tripled.

Like many people around the world, I am fortunate to sit in the shade of a tree planted by Warren Buffett.

38

"Find something you love to do, and you'll never have to work a day in your life."

—HARVEY MACKAY

HARVEY MACKAY is the author of seven *New York Times* best-selling books written to inspire and give advice to people who want to make the most of their professional careers. He has sold approximately ten million copies in eighty countries, and they have been translated into fifty different languages worldwide. Three of his books hit number one and were named by the *New York Times* as the "most inspirational business books of all time."

Born in 1932 in St. Paul, Minnesota, Harvey Mackay has built a career as an author, motivational speaker, and syndicated columnist. He is featured in more than 100 newspapers and magazines.

After graduating from the University of Minnesota, Harvey Mackay took a job selling envelopes for Quality Park Envelope Company. Using his membership and connections made with fellow golfers and business people at Oak Ridge Country Club, he grew his clientele to a substantial level. He was soon named the company's number one salesperson.

In 1959, Harvey Mackay purchased a small, financially distressed envelope manufacturing company that employed twelve people and housed a few folding machines. The direct mail business he named the Mackay Envelope Company became successful over time.

CHAPTER 38

In 1985, the company introduced an innovative new product—the Photopak, an envelope designed to hold processed photo prints. Eight years later, Scott Mitchell joined the company and became Harvey Mackay's business partner, renaming the Photopak division MackayMitchell Photopak. Today, it is the largest North American supplier of photo envelopes. The company employs five hundred employees and produces twenty-five million envelopes daily.

At age 56, Mackay wrote his first book, *Swim with the Sharks without Being Eaten Alive*, which remained on the *New York Times* bestseller list for fifty-four weeks.

In an interview with Nick Kho of the *Mastermind Show*, Harvey Mackay discussed his 1999 book, *Dig Your Well Before You're Thirsty*, in which he addressed the importance of networking—a concept he learned from his father. Networking has been what Harvey Mackay has been doing successfully all of his life. He shared with Kho that, "Every person you meet for the rest of your life goes into a Rolodex file with information on the back of the card about the person. Now," he continued, "here's the key: find a creative way to keep in touch with each person." He went on to say that he has ultimately accumulated twenty million contact names.

After releasing his first book, Harvey Mackay became a professional speaker, with keynote and motivational engagements. One of his primary philosophies has become his company's motto: "Do what you love, love what you do, and deliver more than you promise."

Throughout his career, Harvey Mackay has championed many worthy causes. He sits on the board of the Minnesota Orchestra, and in the 1970s, a Stadium Task Force was developed to construct the Hubert H. Humphrey Metrodome. Harvey Mackay chaired the committee.

In the mid-1980s, due to a decline in attendance, there was a concern that the Minnesota Twins baseball club owner, Calvin Griffith, would sell the team to outside investors and relocate it to another state. Harvey Mackay and other Twin Cities business leaders purchased thousands of Minnesota Twins seat tickets to save the ball club from being sold. Ultimately, a local banker, Carl Pohlad, purchased the team, and it remains in Minnesota.

Harvey Mackay believes that "the biggest room in the world is the room for improvement." He has been instrumental in helping others to reach their career goals.

———— A ————

Like many people around the world, I became a fan of Harvey Mackay's books and his powerful, positive messages. After getting to share the stage with him at an event, I realized that Harvey Mackay not only shared his messages, he lived them. In his quote, *"Find something you love to do, and you'll never have to work a day in your life,"* Harvey Mackay reminds us that nothing takes the place of passion in impacting our performance.

If you pursue a career or profession that is not your passion, you will invariably be competing against people who are pursuing their passion. This is an impossible deficit to overcome as you pursue success. We can't all pursue our passion immediately, but we can pursue our passion inevitably.

39

*"Once you replace negative thoughts with
positive ones, you'll start having positive results."*

—WILLIE NELSON

RECOGNIZED AS ONE OF the most legendary songwriters, singers, and guitarists in country music, Willie Nelson has entertained audiences for decades with his uniquely soothing voice and relaxed stage presence. His music has crossed over many genres, including country, reggae, jazz, pop, blues, folk, and rock.

Along with fellow artists Waylon Jennings, Johnny Cash, and Kris Kristofferson, he was instrumental in spearheading a subgenre of country music. They created a fresh approach known as "outlaw country," which became most popular in the 1970s and early 1980s. The group became known as *The Highwaymen*. Their sound combined blues, honky-tonk, rockabilly, and the era's evolving rock and roll music. More importantly, it defied the traditional Nashville country music sounds from the 1960s and early 1970s by establishing creative freedom for artists.

Born April 29, 1933, in Fort Worth, Texas, Willie Nelson wrote his first song at age 7. His grandfather taught him to play the guitar and, using his talent, joined the John Reycjeck's Bohemian Polka Band when he was 10 years old.

Since that time, Willie Nelson has produced ninety-five studio albums, seventy of them solos and twenty-five collaborations with other artists in various music styles. Though he did not earn much popularity as a singer early in his career, he composed legendary hits for country, rhythm and blues, and other music artists. His song, "Hello Walls," was made famous by country music great Faron Young. One of his most successful ballads was "Crazy," written in 1961. Patsy Cline made the song famous. Willie Nelson recalled, "We went over to Patsy's house…I went in and sang it for her, and she recorded it the next week." "Crazy" became her signature tune until she died in a plane crash two years later.

Written the same week as "Crazy," were "Night Life," popularized by Ray Price, and his first song, "Funny How Time Slips Away," performed by Billy Walker. As for Willie Nelson's well-known recordings, his 1975 album, *Red Headed Stranger*, featured his hit song, "Blue Eyes Crying in the Rain." Fred Rose wrote the music, and Roy Acuff originally recorded it in 1947.

Willie Nelson has appeared in thirty-one movies. In 1979, he appeared in his first film acting role in *Electric Horseman*, followed by his first leading motion picture role, opposite Dyan Cannon, in the 1980 romantic drama *Honeysuckle Rose*. The film debuted his hit song, "On the Road Again." As he recalled to *Uncut* magazine, the song was written on the spur of the moment on an airsickness bag on a flight with the film's movie director, Jerry Schatzberg, and executive producer Sydney Pollack. "They were looking for songs for the movie, and they asked me if I had any ideas. I said, 'What do you want the song to say?' and Sydney said, 'Can it be something about being on the road?' It just started to click.

I said, 'You mean like, on the road again, I can't wait to get on the road again?' They said, 'That's great. What's the melody?' I said, 'I don't know, yet.'" Willie Nelson found the melody, the song became a number one hit, and it won a Grammy in 1980 for Best Country Song. In 2004, *Rolling Stone* ranked it on the "500 Greatest Songs of All Time" list, and in 2011 it was inducted into the Grammy Hall of Fame.

His roles as outlaw Barbarosa in the 1982 Western of the same name, along with Gary Busey, and his 1986 film, *Red Headed Stranger*, brought further notoriety to his acting career.

Though Willie Nelson has toured, along with his sister, Bobbie, most of his career entertaining audiences around the country, he finds time to spend with his children. Many of them have carried the talent torch and made careers in music like their father. His oldest daughter, Lana, played a small part in Willie Nelson's 1986 film, *Red Headed Stranger*.

Though not a music artist, Susie found success as an author. She published an autobiography titled *Heart Worn Memories: A Daughter's Personal Biography of Willie Nelson* in 1987. In it, she paid tribute to her father.

Willie Hugh Jr., known as Billy, had a promising career in music before devastatingly passing on Christmas Day in 1991, at age 33, leaving Willie Nelson heartbroken. In 1994, he released a gospel album in his late son's honor.

Paula toured with her father as a child; and in 2013, sang a father and daughter duet titled, "Have You Ever Seen the Rain?" It was recorded on his duets album titled, *To All the Girls…*, released in honor of his 80th birthday. On it, he sang eighteen duets with female artists including Dolly Parton, Rosanne Cash, Sheryl Crow, and Loretta Lynn, to name a few.

Amy Lee is often seen singing with her father on stage, although she is part of the Folk Uke group.

Lukas is the first-born son of his fourth wife, Annie D'Angelo, and is perhaps the most recognized of Willie Nelson's children. He fronts the band "Lukas Nelson & The Promise of the Real" and performs in his father's band known as the "Family." He is a singer, guitarist, and songwriter. Though no one sings like

Willie Nelson, Lukas performs with the same vocal talent as his father. He is credited with writing music for the 2018 film *A Star is Born*, assisting with the production of the soundtrack, and performing as Bradley Cooper's guitarist in the movie.

His youngest son, Jacob "Micah," often tours with his father and brother, although he heads the band, "Particle Kid." Micah credits his father for his interest and success in music, saying, "He was breaking down barriers and fearlessly doing his thing. For me, to fearlessly do my thing and be myself, I can't think of any other way to respect and honor my dad's legacy."

Willie Nelson had a fifth daughter, Renee, whom he discovered in 2012. The Nelson family has openly welcomed her, her daughter, and granddaughter into their clan.

As an author, Nelson wrote and cowrote more than twenty books, including: *Willie—An Autobiography; Roll Me Up and Smoke Me When I Die—Musings from the Road; It's a Long Story—My Life;* and *Me and Sister Bobbie—True Tales of the Family Band* written by the siblings. With coauthor Turk Pipkin, *Willie Nelson's Letters to America* is a collection of stories, advice, and jokes.

Willie Nelson will forever be remembered for his charitable contributions to "Farm Aid" that began in 1985 and the "USA for Africa" fundraiser. His concert event in 2004 raised $75,000 for UNICEF to aid the Indian Ocean earthquake, and the concert in Kokua raised $1.6 million for victims of the 2011 Tohoku earthquake and tsunami in Japan.

Willie Nelson is well-known for his support of legalizing marijuana. In 2015, he launched a marijuana supply company, "Willie's Reserve," and remains on the advisory board of the National Organization for the Reform of Marijuana Laws (NORML). Environmentally conscious, he owns the biodiesel brand "Willie Nelson Biodiesel," made from vegetable oil.

Over the years, Willie Nelson's fashion has shifted from his clean-shaven, suit and tie-wearing persona of the 1950s and 1960s to the unconventional signature style he adopted in 1972. He was recognized for his cinnamon and salt-colored braids that hung to his waist with a bandana wrapped snugly around his forehead. He continues to entertain and connect with audiences wearing a red, white, and blue lanyard around his neck that attaches to his nylon-stringed Martin guitar he calls "Trigger." In 2010, he surprised fans by cutting his braids in what he called on his website the "Haircut heard around the World."

Willie Nelson's stage performance has stood the test of time, and his concerts continue to be must-see events as he tours from city to city year after year. His music plays on jukeboxes across the country, and his songs remain favorites for karaoke enthusiasts. Willie Nelson's rustic appearance is as much a part of his charisma as his captivating voice. When he is not performing, he finds time for a relaxing round of golf, dominos, chess, and card games with his friends in the tropical paradise of Hawaii.

———— A ————

I first met Willie Nelson at a mutual friend's birthday party. I found him to be friendly and engaging, but I really became impressed with him when I met with him after several of his concerts. He simply loved the process of entertaining crowds of people, and he was definitely at home and in his element. He stood for literally several hours meeting and greeting fans. He treated every one of them as if they were the only person who had come to his show that night.

Willie told me that once he finally broke through and started achieving success, the entertainment industry media proclaimed him to be an overnight sensation. He laughingly reminded me that at that point in his career he had been playing for twenty long years on the road, but he always knew he would make it. In his quote, *"Once you replace negative thoughts with positive ones, you'll start having positive results,"* Willie reminds us all that our attitude controls our actions, and our actions control our results.

40

"It ain't over till it's over."

—YOGI BERRA

YOGI BERRA WAS BORN LORENZO PIETRO BERRA on May 12, 1925, in St. Louis, Missouri. His parents were Italian immigrants who came to the United States for a better life. Determined to Americanize Lorenzo Pietro's name, the English translation became Lawrence Peter. Unable to pronounce this adaptation with their distinctive accents, his family merely called him "Lawdie." But one hot summer afternoon, Lawdie Berra forever became known as Yogi Berra.

It happened when a group of boyhood friends went to the movies to see a travel log of India. Playing on the screen was the story of a Hindu Fakir who reached the level of Yogi. Seeing the holy man sitting with his arms folded and his knees crossed, it occurred to one of the boys, the future eight-season Major League Baseball outfielder, Jack Maguire, that the Yogi resembled Lawdie Berra in one of his pondering moods. Lawdie Berra became known as Yogi Berra to family, friends, colleagues, and fans from that day forward.

Yogi Berra had developed his athletic talents by playing sports with his three older brothers, along with close neighborhood friends Jack Maguire and Joe Garagiola (senior), who became a prominent St. Louis Cardinal baseball catcher.

After serving at Normandy, France, Berra earned a Purple Heart as a gunner's mate in the United States Navy during World War II. Yogi Berra began his legendary Major League Baseball career, signing with the New York Yankees. He received the number "8" jersey, and he proved to be a power hitter. Skillfully, he hit a home run in his first career at-bat and played with the team for eighteen seasons. He held a solid defensive reputation as the team's catcher throughout his tenure.

Yogi Berra retired after the 1963 season, but went on to coach the New York Mets ball club in 1965. He remained with the team for the next decade, becoming the team's manager during the last four years of service. Yogi Berra returned to the New York Yankees team in 1976. There, he coached for eight seasons and managed for the final two before signing as a coach with the Houston Astros until the season's end in 1989.

Ultimately, Yogi Berra played in or coached twenty-one World Series games, thirteen attained victory. His career batting average was .285, hitting 358 home runs and 1,430 RBIs. Impressively, he played 148 consecutive games without an error, became a three-time American League Most Valuable Player, and was an All-Star fifteen times in his career. He played home-plate catcher in the 1956 World Series during pitcher Don Larson's perfect game. After the victory, Yogi Berra leaped into Don Larson's arms. The celebration was caught on film, and it became an iconic image in baseball history.

Yogi Berra was notorious for his malapropisms and his brief and ironic statements. He would mistakenly use an incorrect word in place of one similar-sounding, or he coined a phrase that either contradicted or restated itself, resulting in a humorous delivery and undying quote. They remain in history as "Yogi-isms." Yogi Berra once both denied and confirmed that "The funniest thing about the things that I said was that I didn't say half of them. Then again, I might have said 'em, but you never know."

During an apparent disappointing season, a reporter asked about the team's chances of coming out of the slump. Always the optimist with a can-do attitude, Yogi Berra would find a reason for positive certainty and hope even when all seemed lost. It was at this time that he uttered his most notorious Yogi-ism—"It ain't over till it's over." Other known malapropisms were, "It's like déjà vu all over again," "We made too many wrong mistakes," "You can observe a lot just by watching," and "Baseball is 90 percent mental. The other half is physical."

When giving Joe Garagiola directions to his house in New Jersey, he said, "When you come to the fork in the road, take it." While this sounded ridiculous, either direction chosen would have landed Joe at his house, as each point of entry circled and his home was at the halfway mark.

Traditionally, on the team's trips to the Twin Cities in Minnesota to play against the Twins, the players went to Charlie's Café Exceptionale in downtown Minneapolis. It was the city's most talked-about dining establishment at the time, and the place became so popular that it was consistently busy. Once when asked by a team member if he was going to go to Charlie's, Berra answered, "Nobody goes there anymore. It's too crowded."

When Yogi Berra was named manager of the New York Yankees in 1963, baseball writer Robert Lipsyte said of his zinger quotes, "He has continued to allow people to regard him as an amiable clown because it brings him quick acceptance, despite ample proof, on-field and off, that he is intelligent, shrewd, and opportunistic." Though he only had an eighth-grade education, Yogi Berra was not a clown or buffoon. He was a clever businessman, strategic ballplayer, coach and manager, and a genius of wit.

Yogi Berra died on September 22, 2015, at the age of 90 due to natural causes. His ashes were interred next to Carmen's, his wife of sixty-five years. To honor his contribution to the New York Yankees, the team donned the number "8" patch on their uniforms in his honor. The Empire State Building in New York City was illuminated in blue and white pinstripes on September 23, and American flags were lowered to half-staff in tribute. Teams throughout the country held a moment of silence for the Baseball Hall of Famer. Sadly, his boyhood and long-time friend, Joe Garagiola Sr., died six months later.

Opened in 1998, the Yogi Berra Museum and Learning Center was established. It was designed to teach children the importance of sportsmanship and showcase priceless artifacts and game-used items, including the mitt he wore when he caught the last out in the 1956 World Series. On October 8, 2014, vandals broke in and stole nine of Yogi Berra's World Series championship rings and two MVP plaques that were on display. Though the police offered a $5,000 cash reward, the items were never recovered.

On October 27, 2014, it was announced that exact replicas of the items would be graciously replaced by donations from the Commissioner, Allan Selig, Major League Baseball, the New York Yankees, and the New York Mets. Together, they donated several new items to add to the collection, "ensuring that the museum will be an even better place for fans to visit in honor of Yogi's legacy."

I have always been a baseball fan. As a blind person myself, I enjoy listening to a game on the radio almost every night throughout the season. My father was a Minor League Baseball player, so I've always been intrigued by All-Star caliber players who made their mark on the game. Yogi Berra's statistics as a Hall of Fame baseball player speak for themselves, and his enduring quotes also speak for themselves.

I've often said, even as a blind person I could get a hit off of the best pitcher in the Major Leagues if you will allow me to alter just one of the rules of baseball. Instead of three strikes, if you will give me an unlimited number of opportunities to swing the bat at the baseball, eventually and inevitably, I will get a hit because, as Yogi reminds us, until I quit I'm still in the game and at the plate. As long as we're still swinging at the ball, we can succeed.

41

"You can never have too many friends."

—JAMES GARNER

JAMES GARNER came into our world as James Scott Bumgarner on April 7, 1928, in Norman, Oklahoma. After contracting with Warner Brothers in 1956, the studio changed his name, arguing that no man can become famous with the word *bum* in his name. As James "Garner," he found success in film and television roles with his ruggedly handsome looks, contagious smile, and endearing southern wit and charm.

When asked about his comedic acting style, he said, "I don't do comedy. I do humor." He lightheartedly mused, "I've always kept my tongue in my cheek and a twinkle in my eye because I want people to laugh with me, not at me. I don't want them to think I take this play-acting too seriously." James Garner brought a unique and memorable approach to delivering a subtle mix of sarcasm and humor to his characters.

James Garner's laid-back performances made his acting look rather natural, and he mastered the art of reacting in a scene rather than acting. He once credited his style to the talented actor Henry Fonda, saying that he spent hours watching how he moved. "It was an experience just watching the way he sat down," he said. "I copied much of what I saw in Fonda when I made the film *Support Your Local Gunfighter.*" Playing good-natured character roles as cowboy, lawman, gambler, detective, and racecar driver elevated him to stardom.

Before stardom, James Garner shied from any recognition and preferred to remain out of the limelight. As he viewed it, acting was a job—a source of income—rather than pursuing attention. He had a reputation for traveling about working town to town, job after job. "I traveled a lot in those days," he said. At age 16, near the end of World War II, he headed to California and joined the United States Merchant Marines. That job did not pan out, as he had developed chronic seasickness and was discharged a few months later. "I didn't stay at any one thing very long. I guess I must have had five or six dozen jobs of one kind or another when I was a kid. I just couldn't make up my mind what I wanted to do, but I knew there was something for me somewhere, and one day I would find it."

Find it, he did. In 1954, he began his acting career when his friend and well-known producer Paul Gregory got him a nonspeaking role in the Broadway production of *The Caine Mutiny Court Martial.* James Garner promised himself a five-year commitment to make it in Hollywood or give up the notion. While on set, he honed the craft of acting by reading lines with other actors and observing their behaviors on stage.

His first memorable role was starring in the Western comedy television series *Maverick* that aired from 1957 to 1962. James Garner played the likable money-loving, traveling gambler Bret Maverick with his natural Oklahoman accent. He and his on-screen brother, Bart Maverick, played by Jack Kelly, worked together each week to get through an elaborate swindling scheme to get even with someone who had robbed them.

James Garner's off-screen older brother, Jack Garner, who also changed his name from Bumgarner, played supporting roles in sixty episodes of his detective series *The Rockford Files*. James Garner played James "Jim" Scott Rockford. It aired from 1974 to 1980.

Besides his acclaimed television roles, James Garner played in forty-seven movies, many starring with countless well-known celebrities, including his last performance in *The Ultimate Gift*, based on the book of the same name written by Jim Stovall. In the film, James Garner plays a billionaire grandfather, Red Stevens, who appears in a video at the reading of his will. He conditionally leaves his overindulged grandson his fortune. First, he must set out on a journey in which the young man must learn life lessons and self-discovery to earn the ultimate gift—the gift of caring for others.

In 1966, James Garner starred in the fictional drama *Grand Prix* that chronicles four Formula One race car drivers. The film sets the stage for his lifelong interest in both on-road and off-road auto racing. From 1967 to 1969, he owned the American International Racing team. James Garner placed in the Banshee, a vehicle built for him by fellow Hall of Fame Inductee Vic Hickey. Driving the car, he won the Riverside Grand Prix, and on other occasions, he placed the car, winning in the top five. On three occasions, James Garner drove the pace car to kick off the Indianapolis 500 races in Indianapolis, Indiana. In 1978, he was one of the inaugural inductees into the Off-Road Motorsports Hall of Fame.

In 2006, a 10-foot-tall bronze statue of James Garner as Bret Maverick was unveiled in downtown Norman, Oklahoma. He was present at the ceremony in his hometown.

James Garner suffered a stroke in 2008 and remained in poor health until he died on July 19, 2014, of a heart attack at age 86. His legacy lives on in his movies and television programs. He is not forgotten.

—— A ——

As the author of more than fifty books and having eight of my novels turned into movies, I've had many exciting milestones in my career. But none of them prove to be greater than having James Garner star in *The Ultimate Gift*, which was the first movie based on one of my books. Like most Americans, I grew up watching James Garner play Maverick and Rockford in those iconic TV series. But only when I met him and got to work with him did I come to understand that he embodied the most loveable elements of those characters.

So many lines I wrote for my lead character, Red Stevens, were given new power and significance because of the way Mr. Garner delivered them. He turned a complex character facing a difficult situation into someone the audience could understand, respect, and want to have as a friend. Mr. Garner understood that the best way to have a friend is to be a friend.

42

*"All our dreams come true if we
have the courage to pursue them."*

—WALT DISNEY

WHEN ASKED WHERE to find the "Happiest Place on Earth," many might say, "Disney." Others may not say Disney, but suddenly find its theme song, "When You Wish Upon a Star," begin to loop in their minds, thanks to Walt Disney and his older brother, Roy Oliver Disney. The Disney name will forever be linked to amusement, fantasy, and imagination.

Walter Elias Disney was born in Chicago, Illinois, on December 5, 1901, and at age 4, his family moved to Missouri. He was the fourth of five children. He was not an attentive student but constantly sketched and drew as a youngster. His interest heightened when he was paid to draw a horse belonging to a retired neighbor doctor. Some years later, his family moved back to Chicago, and he attended McKinley High School. While there, he was a cartoonist for the school newspaper, and he attended night courses at the Chicago Academy of Fine Arts. At 16, he dropped out of high school.

April 6, 1917, three years into World War I, the United States Congress declared war on Germany, and Walt Disney joined the Red Cross Ambulance Corps to serve his country. He had forged his birth certificate to reflect that he met the minimum age requirement of 17 and was sent to France in late

1918. Though the Armistice Treaty calling for a cease-fire had been signed before he enlisted, he remained in the service until discharged in 1919.

With the dream of becoming a cartoonist and an interest in animation, in 1922, he opened the short-lived film studio "Laugh-O-Gram." After its financial failure a year later, Walt Disney decided to move to Hollywood, and along with his brother, Roy, he formed Disney Brothers Studio. Walt Disney led the company's creative development, and Roy maintained the business and financial side of the partnership.

At the Disney Brothers Studio, Walt Disney developed the iconic cartoon character Mickey Mouse. Originally dubbed Mortimer Mouse, the company's ink artist and Walt Disney's wife, Lillian Bounds, determined that the name "Mickey" was better suited for the lovable rodent. Mickey made his debut in 1928 in the short film titled *Steamboat Willie*, and he soon became a star. Children adored him, and the Mickey Mouse Clubs were born. The mouse and his big-eared image became well-known on merchandise and comics. Mickey spoke his first words on the screen in 1929, saying, "Hot dog, hot dog." Not pleased with the original voice, Walt Disney lent his voice to the character until he became too busy to continue doing so in 1947.

Walt Disney had a fascination with trains. As a young man in Kansas City, he briefly sold newspapers and snacks aboard the train. His passion grew, and in the late 1940s, he constructed a one-eighth scale steam locomotive with miniature cars designed to tote passengers. It was a hobby that soothed the stressors of his day. When he moved into the Holmby Hills district of Los Angeles in 1950, he laid a half-mile track around his property, dressed in an engineer's costume, and gave visitors rides. He named the train "Carolwood Pacific Railroad." Though Walt Disney retired the train, his affection for them continued.

Walt Disney had long dreamt of building a theme park that would reflect all that was the magic of Disney. It had to be family-oriented—a happy place for children and adults. And so it was—one year and one day from the start of construction, "Disneyland" opened. Fifteen thousand guests were invited to the grand opening on July 17, 1955. It was a magical affair that was broadcast live on the ABC network. With a population of 165 million at the time, 70 million people tuned into the weekly program that featured the 160-acre, $17 million theme park that stood in the orange groves of Anaheim, California. Walt Disney had borrowed against his life insurance, sold his vacation property, and took the ABC network as one-third owner in the project to make it happen.

The park featured four points of interest—Frontierland, Adventureland, Fantasyland, and Tomorrowland. Actor and future president of the United States Ronald Reagan cohosted the event alongside Walt Disney. Sammy Davis Jr. and Frank Sinatra were spotted speeding in cars around the miniature motorway ride called the "Autopia" and lent notoriety to the event.

The event was equally magical to the millions who watched from their living rooms.

The event, however, was not without mishap. While 15,000 people received invitations, 28,154 attended. The park was over capacity due to counterfeit tickets and people selling admissions over the back fence for five dollars per person. Parts of the park were unfinished, making those areas off-limits to guests, some of the rides were not in working condition yet, and a gas leak forced Fantasyland to close for the day. It was dubbed "Black Sunday."

All was not lost, though. The park was, in reality, a success. Within one month, modifications were complete, and everything ran smoothly. Sixty years later, more than 750 million people went through the turnstiles of Disneyland.

In 1965, Walt Disney had a vision for a second theme park. It would be called "Disney World," later renamed "Walt Disney World." The site selected was Orlando, Florida, and it would be larger and more elaborate than Disneyland. It would be a new type of city that people could enjoy and learn from an environment of futuristic innovations and technologies. He called the creation the "Experimental Prototype Community of Tomorrow," also known as EPCOT. It would, as he described, "take its cue from the new ideas and new technologies that are now emerging from the creative centers of American industry. It will be a community of tomorrow that will never be completed but will always be introducing, testing, and demonstrating new materials and systems. And EPCOT will always be a showcase to the world for the ingenuity and imagination of American free enterprise." Disney World opened its turnstiles to the public on October 1, 1971. Unfortunately, Walt Disney died before the project was complete.

Walt Disney had been a heavy smoker most of his life, preferring the unfiltered cigarettes. In November 1966, he was diagnosed with lung cancer. His treatment was unsuccessful, and on December 15, ten days after his 65th birthday, he died. After his death, Roy Disney continued to oversee the construction of Disney World. In tribute to his late brother, he renamed the theme park "Walt Disney World." Walt Disney's love for trains is apparent in the modern-day locomotives that circle the theme parks.

In the *American National Biography*, Mark Langer, former Associate Professor of Carleton University, writes of Walt Disney:

Disney remains the central figure in animation history. Through technological innovations and alliances with governments and corporations, he transformed a minor studio in a marginal form of communications into a multinational leisure industry giant. Despite his critics, his vision of a modern corporate utopia as an extension of traditional American values has possibly gained greater currency in the years after his death.

Walt Disney's vision continues to put smiles on the faces of children and adults alike. In February 1960, Walt Disney was honored with two stars on the Hollywood Walk of Fame. One was for his contribution to motion pictures, and the other was for television. Mickey Mouse was given a motion picture star of his own in 1978.

— A —

In my novel, *The Ultimate Gift*—which was the basis for the 20th Century Fox movie of the same name, I recounted a legendary incident in the life of Walt Disney. In his later years, he was hospitalized with a condition that eventually took his life. Literally on his deathbed, Walt Disney tacked his drawings for future attractions at the Disney parks to the ceiling so he could lie in his hospital bed and dream about his vision for the future. More than one executive told of Walt Disney asking them to lie on the bed beside him so they both could review the plans on the ceiling.

Walt Disney had the courage to pursue his dreams, and his vision for the future overshadowed any challenges or obstacles he might have faced in the present moment.

43

"The measure of who we are
is what we do with what we have."

—VINCE LOMBARDI

VINCENT THOMAS LOMBARDI will forever be remembered as the head coach of the Green Bay Packers, beginning at a time when the struggling National Football League (NFL) football team from Wisconsin needed a bold, determined, and relentless taskmaster to lead them to victory.

The oldest of five children, he was born on June 11, 1913, in Brooklyn, New York, to Italian ancestry parents who instilled a strong Christian faith in their family. Vince Lombardi attended church service 365 days a year throughout his life, faithfully rising early to attend mass.

His father, Enrico, who preferred to be called "Harry," owned a butcher shop in Manhattan's Meatpacking District. Harry worked hard and played hard and expected his children to learn and appreciate the merits of both. As a constant reminder of his philosophy, Harry, who was highly tattooed, had the letters of the words *w-o-r-k* and *p-l-a-y* symbolically tattooed on the tops of his fingers—one word on each hand. Following his father's example, Vince Lombardi possessed a strong work ethic and dedicated his life to a career that blended work and play. His life focused on faith, family, and football—not necessarily in that order.

After graduating from the eighth grade, Vince Lombardi enrolled in the Cathedral Preparatory Seminary. It was a six-year secondary program designed to prepare young men for the priesthood. The school offered two sports programs—baseball and basketball. Though he loved playing sports, he did not excel at either of them due to his lack of athletic abilities in those sports and his poor eyesight. After four years at the school, he decided not to become a priest. He enrolled at St. Francis Preparatory, where he played fullback for the Terriers' football team. In football, he proved to be an exceptional athlete, and he was an aggressive player. His talent earned him a spot on the All-City football team, and in 1933 he was offered a football scholarship to Fordham University to play for the Rams, a nationally ranked college team.

The team's strength was in its offensive line, which consisted of seven men—one center, two guards, two tackles, and two ends. As right guard, Vince Lombardi weighed in at 180 pounds and stood 5'8" tall. He became one of the team's star players. Halfway through the 1936 season, the team was undefeated and on the brink of its most outstanding season ever. To build excitement, the school's publicist, Timothy Cohane, dubbed the extraordinary offensive lineup as the "Seven Blocks of Granite" to rival Notre Dame's famous "Four Horsemen." The nickname stuck, and a monument was erected on the college campus in honor of its Seven Blocks of Granite.

With a degree in business, Vince Lombardi was not confident of his future. He decided to give law school a try, but after only a semester, he dropped out and went to work as a chemist for a year.

In 1939, he received a phone call from a former classmate who offered him a teaching position at St. Cecilia High School in Englewood, New Jersey. Excitedly for him, the job provided an opportunity to coach the football team. As assistant to his friend's head coaching position, he had additional responsibilities. He taught Latin, chemistry, physics, and physical education and remained at the school as coach for eight years—the last five years he served as head coach. The football team became recognized as the top football team in the nation.

Vince Lombardi's coaching style was strict, and the players were required to follow his rigid, disciplinarian rules. There was always room for improvement, he thought, so he studied the sport intensely. He broke down the field plays systematically and logically. He believed his players could not play well if they did not learn the game, so he taught them each choreographed play, frequently losing his temper when a player consistently made errors. He imposed a harsh regime and demanded total dedication from his men. Vince Lombardi was known for his temperament, and he kicked and threw things in anger. Some of his players appreciated his methods and enjoyed playing under his instruction. Others complained of his rigorous approach to the game. Being a winning coach, however, such dramatics were generally tolerated.

In 1947, he returned to his alma mater, Fordham University, to coach the freshman and later the varsity football teams. To his dismay, he was assigned to the basketball team as well. Not knowing much about basketball, Vince Lombardi read books from the school's library to teach himself the game's strategies.

Following his tenure with the university, he coached at the U.S. Military Academy at West Point, New York, for five seasons and then moved to the NFL's New York Giants.

In the winter of 1959, Vince Lombardi packed up his family and moved to what has been referred to as the Siberia of the NFL. As his daughter, Susan, tells the story, "The big announcement...'We are moving to Green Bay, Wisconsin.' I'm going, 'Where's Wisconsin?' So the next day, my father comes home with a map. He said, 'This is the state of Wisconsin,' and he's looking. 'Green Bay? It isn't on the map.' And I say, 'Well, I'm not moving any place that's not on the map.' He said, 'When I am done, it will be on that map, and you'll know exactly, Susan, where you live.'"

Vince Lombardi kept that promise to his daughter. He did not doubt his ability to lead the Green Bay Packers to victory, and he accepted the position with the contingency of being given total control. He told the executive committee, "I want it understood that I am in complete command here." With his strong faith and coaching skills, he brought the Green Bay Packers to victory by winning five National Football League Championships, including the first two Super Bowls—1966 and 1967. He was named NFL Coach of the Year in 1959 and 1961.

In Lombardi's words, "I think one of the things that made America great is to try to be the best at everything that they do. And the best, again, is signified by winning."

Vince Lombardi had suffered from intestinal problems as early as 1967. Friends, family, and players had long encouraged him to seek medical treatment, but he refused to undergo a proctoscopy exam. By June 24, 1970, he was admitted to Georgetown University Hospital in Washington, DC, for tests. He was diagnosed with fast-growing cancer. It was terminal. His family, friends, clergy, players, and former players were at his bedside to say goodbye. On September 3, 1970, Vince Lombardi died. He was 57.

Before Super Bowl V in 1970, the winning trophy was renamed from the "World Professional Football Championship Trophy" to the "Vince Lombardi Trophy" in his honor. The trophy, valued at more than $10,000, is presented as a permanent symbol of excellence.

—— A ——

Vince Lombardi's words remind us that we cannot compare ourselves to others. We can only compare ourselves to the potential we have and the person we should be. Vince Lombardi is among the handful of best coaches of all time in the National Football League.

The respect for him is evident in the fact that the winner of the Super Bowl each year receives the Lombardi trophy. Vince Lombardi was never the greatest football player, but he may have gotten more out of his limited talent than anyone else playing at that time. His championship teams were not always made up of the best players, but they were definitely made up of players who played their best.

Social media has created an environment where we are all worried about what everyone else thinks of us; when in the final analysis, the only opinion that should matter is the one we have of ourselves compared to who we know we should be.

44

*"In all chaos there is a cosmos,
in all disorder a secret order."*

—CARL G. JUNG

CARL GUSTAV JUNG, referred to as "C.G." by all who knew him, was born Karl Gustav Jung. Though given the modern spelling of Karl at birth, he later changed it. He was born the fourth, though the first living child to his parents on July 26, 1875, in Kesswil, on Lake Constance, in the Swiss canton of Thurgau in Switzerland. He was a Swiss psychoanalyst and psychiatrist who pioneered analytical psychology. His work continues to influence many fields of study, such as anthropology, archaeology, literature, philosophy, psychology, and some religious studies.

As a child, Carl Jung was an introverted young man and enjoyed spending time alone. Though he had a sister, Johanna Gertrud Jung, nine years his junior, he preferred to sit in isolation to explore his thoughts. His mother was eccentric, and she gravitated toward depression and isolation from the family. The relationship with his father was far better.

Like his mother, Carl Jung believed he had two personalities— the contemporary persona and that of an archaic 18th-century persona. The contemporary personality or "Personality Number 1," as he referred to it was that of a schoolboy living in his time. The archaic persona, known as "Personality Number 2," was a dignified gentleman from the past who was authoritative and influential. This belief greatly influenced his future theories.

CHAPTER 44

When Jung was 12, a schoolmate pushed him so hard that he fell and briefly lost consciousness. As a result, he thought that he would no longer have to attend school by fainting. Believing it to be true, he fainted whenever he walked to school or had to do his homework. Ultimately, this practice kept him home from school for the next six months. Until one day, he overheard his father speaking to someone about his son's future ability to support himself, as they had suspected he must have epilepsy.

Carl Jung sensed from the conversation that his family was nearing poverty. As a result, he realized that he must buckle down and achieve academic excellence to avoid such a situation. Immediately, he began studying his Latin grammar lessons. Eventually, he overcame the urge to faint and did not have another spell. He later recalled that the event "was when I learned what a neurosis is."

In 1895, Carl Jung pursued a degree in psychiatry and medicine at the University of Basel, founded in 1460 in Basel, Switzerland. It has a reputation nationally for its outstanding achievements in research and teaching. The thought of combining the biological and spiritual elements to his profession intrigued him. He had developed a strong moral sense from his childhood home life, so his first inclination was to become a preacher or minister, as many family members were clergymen. Though his real passion was to study archaeology, the university did not offer such courses, and funds were unavailable to venture outside his community. He soon abandoned the idea of both of those areas of study and focused on the subconscious mind.

In the early 20th century, Carl Jung first became a physician primarily practicing in Zurich, Switzerland, before entering the emerging field of psychoanalysis and psychiatry. As a psychotherapist and psychiatrist, he created a unique area of study known as analytical psychology. "Individualization" was at the core of his theory. It was a process of differentiating an individual through the conscious and unconscious mind. In his analysis, it was the central element of human development.

From 1913 to 1921, Dr. Carl Jung published three significant papers. Two essays were on "Analytical Psychology," which summarized the basic ideas for his later work, and the third reviewed "Psychological Types." The Jungian terms, as they were called, stated that there are two basic classifications or personality types relating to "introversion" and "extroversion." These terms have become part of the language of psychological typology.

A person's typology significantly influences how they observe and interact with the world around them. The introverted person is characterized as being self-involved, withdrawn, and occupied with one's "inner world." At the same time, the extrovert term relates to the world through social interaction and involvement by being "outgoing" with outside interests.

Also known as Jungian psychology, Carl Jung's concepts were synchronicity or coexistence, archetypal phenomena or stereotypical, collective unconscious, psychological complex, and four major archetypes: 1) the "persona," conveying how we present ourselves to the world; 2) the "shadow," consisting of the sex and life instincts; 3) the "anima or animus," referring to the feminine image in the male psyche and the male image in the female psyche; and 4) the "self," which represents the unified unconsciousness and consciousness of an individual.

During Carl Jung's intellectual developmental years, he and Sigmund Freud influenced each other. Although they possessed many of the same fundamental psychological beliefs and ideas, they did not always agree. Many times, at the height of their friendship, they met to discuss their views. Once, they talked for twelve hours nonstop. Each man told the other his dreams. In turn, each gave his interpretations and presumed significance.

Carl Jung became a full professor of medical psychology at the University of Basel in 1943, but he suffered a heart attack the following year and retired. He was also known as an artist, craftsman, builder, and prolific writer throughout his life. Many of his works were not published until after his death, and much of his writings are still awaiting publication. Among his works was a book published in 1959 titled *Flying Saucers: A Modern Myth of Things Seen in the Skies*. In it, he analyzed the archetypal meaning and possible psychological significance of the reported observations of UFOs.

In 1961, Carl Jung's final contribution, along with various associates, was to the book *Man and His Symbols* entitled "Approaching the Unconscious." It was, ultimately, published three years after his death. He died on June 6, 1961, in Küsnacht, Switzerland.

I consider Dr. Carl Jung to be among a handful of people that I think of as universal human beings. Universal human beings include individuals such as Leonardo da Vinci and Benjamin Franklin who excelled in multiple fields. Carl Jung, in addition to being a pioneer psychiatrist, was a philosopher, a thought leader, and someone whose work has become the basis for much of the modern-day success training in areas of business and personal development.

His quote, *"In all chaos there is a cosmos, in all disorder a secret order,"* reminds us that life can seem chaotic and out of control, but periodically on our life journey, we reach a plateau and break through the clouds so we can consider where we are and observe where we've been. On these occasions, the seeming chaos of our past takes on a divine order and we come to understand that the only way we could have arrived at our destination was to follow the path that we took.

45

*"Nobody cares how much you know
until they know how much you care."*

—THEODORE ROOSEVELT

THEODORE ROOSEVELT JR., often referred to by his initials T.R.
or the nickname Teddy, which name he did not particularly
care for, was a New York governor. Later he became the 26th
president of the United States at age 42. While serving as the
25th vice president, the assassination of President William
McKinley elevated him to the commander in chief. After com-
pleting the remaining three years and six months of President
William McKinley's second term, Theodore Roosevelt served a
full second four-year term in office. He remains the youngest
person to assume the office of the presidency, and his was the
first president's voice to be recorded for posterity. To his credit,
Theodore Roosevelt was known as a statesman, conservationist,
naturalist, war hero, sports enthusiast, and he inspired the
cuddly "Teddy Bear" stuffed toy.

He attended Harvard University, and his book *The Naval
War of 1812*, published the same year, established his reputation
as a well-educated historian and a well-known writer. Theodore
Roosevelt published more than twenty-five books on history,
biology, geography, philosophy, foreign policy, national parks,
and his autobiographies: the four-volume book, *The Winning
of the West*, and his book titled *Rough Riders*. Though he also

attended Columbia Law School, he did not obtain a law degree. Instead, he pursued a life in politics.

Born the second of four children to a socially prominent family in Manhattan, New York, on October 27, 1858, Theodore Roosevelt was a sickly child with debilitating asthma for which there was no known cure. He suffered from frequent attacks, and his father often took him on carriage rides to clear his lung. Being homeschooled, he could devote time and energy to conquering his health problem by applying himself to a "strenuous lifestyle," as he termed it in his speech in Chicago, Illinois, on April 10, 1899, while serving as governor.

In his speech, Theodore Roosevelt remarked, "I wish to preach, not the doctrine of ignoble [inferior] ease, but the doctrine of the strenuous life, the life of toil and effort, of labor and strife; to preach that highest form of success which comes, not to the man who desires mere easy peace, but to the man who does not shrink from danger, from hardship, or from bitter toil, and who out of these wins the splendid ultimate triumph." These were words that Theodore Roosevelt lived by throughout his life. He believed that inactive people, who do not embody a strenuous lifestyle, do not live meaningful lives.

Theodore Roosevelt developed a passion for the outdoors at an early age. His favorite activities included boxing, tennis, hiking, swimming, rowing, polo, horseback riding, bird-watching, taxidermy, and big game hunting. He found strength in exercising regularly, and remembered his father's advice, "Take care of your morals first, your health next, and finally your studies."

Theodore Roosevelt was a strong man and demonstrated his stamina when, in 1912, during a campaign speech in Milwaukee, Wisconsin, a man stalking him for weeks appeared at the rally and shot him once in the chest, point-blank range. The fifty-page document containing his speech, "Progressive Cause Greater Than Any Individual," had been folded twice and tucked into his breast pocket. The speech, along with his metal glasses case, slowed the bullet and saved his life. The shell remained lodged in his chest muscle for the rest of his life. Theodore Roosevelt delivered the 90-minute speech that day in his blood-soaked shirt. His opening comment to the crowd was, "Ladies and gentlemen, I don't know whether you fully understand that I have been shot, but it takes more than that to kill a Bull Moose." The Bull Moose became the iconic symbol of his political party.

Theodore Roosevelt had a lifelong interest in zoology. When he was 7 years old, he saw a dead seal at the local market. He obtained its head and learned how to preserve animal skins, stuffing and mounting them in lifelike arrangements. Along with two cousins, he formed the "Roosevelt Museum of Natural History" in his bedroom. The exhibit consisted of twelve specimens he had killed or caught to study. Some of his collection is on display at the Smithsonian in Washington, DC. At merely 9 years old, he wrote "The Natural History of Insects," recounting his observations.

At the invitation of Mississippi Governor Andrew H. Longing in 1902, Theodore Roosevelt attended a hunting trip near Onward, Mississippi. While all the others in the expedition were successful, he did not spot one bear. His assistants, thinking they were helpful, captured and tied a black bear to a willow tree and suggested Theodore Roosevelt shoot it. He refused, saying he viewed killing in such a manner to be unsportsmanlike.

News of the event quickly spread, and articles popped up in newspapers throughout the country recounting the big game hunter's refusal to kill the bear. Political cartoonist Clifford Berryman read the article that appeared in the *Washington Post* and satirized the event with a cartoon depiction of Theodore Roosevelt holding his hand out in defiance of shooting the animal. The caption read, "Drawing the line in Mississippi."

Seeing Clifford Berryman's cartoon, candy shop owner Morris Michtom and his wife got the idea to create a stuffed toy bear, naming it the "Teddy's Bear." Once he received permission from Theodore Roosevelt to use his name, the couple began mass-producing the Teddy Bear.

Theodore Roosevelt cared deeply about the nation's landscape and wildlife. He promoted its conservation using his presidential authority or executive order beginning in 1901 to establish 150 national forests, 51 federal bird reserves, 4 national game preserves, 5 national parks, and 18 national monuments on over 230 million acres of public land.

In a 1910 speech in Osawatomie, Kansas, Roosevelt said,

> There is a delight in the hardy life of the open. There
> are no words that can tell the hidden spirit of the
> wilderness that can reveal its mystery, its melancholy,
> and its charm. The nation behaves well if it treats
> the natural resources as assets which it must turn over
> to the next generation increased and not impaired
> in value.

Theodore Roosevelt died suddenly on January 6, 1919, of a coronary embolism at age 60. He will forever be remembered as a progressive movement leader and champion of his "Square Deal" domestic political policies. In his words, "The principles for which we stand are the principles of fair play and a square deal for every man and every woman in the United States: A square deal politically, a square deal in matters social and industrial." He promised average citizens of the United States fairness, trust-busting of monopolistic industries, such as the railroads and oil companies, and he was the driving force for pure food and drugs.

Theodore Roosevelt was particularly known for what he called the "Bully Pulpit," which allowed him to publicly express his beliefs and opinions by addressing many people at once to openly say what was right, what was wrong, and where the nation was heading. He shared insight regarding his life, saying, "No man has had a happier life than I have led; a happier life in every way."

In 1927, President Calvin Coolidge approved the colossal carving by American sculpture John Gutzon Borglum into the granite face of Mount Rushmore in the Black Hills near Keystone, South Dakota. Sometimes referred to as the "Shrine of Democracy," the monument depicted the face of Theodore Roosevelt, along with those of Thomas Jefferson, George Washington, and Abraham Lincoln. Since 1960, nearly two million people have visited the Mount Rushmore Memorial annually.

— A —

Whether he was an officer leading soldiers into battle, an athlete, an outdoorsman, or a world leader, Theodore Roosevelt was the epitome of what my grandfather called a "man's man." His epic speech, "In the Arena," has stood the test of time and remains a powerful reminder that the world belongs to the man or woman who attempts to do great things and perseveres regardless of short-term outcomes. This image of President Roosevelt makes his quote regarding caring for others even more powerful and poignant. We all want to make a difference in the world and help others. But it begins with caring, and sometimes just showing that we care can be the greatest help we can offer.

In our world today, when it's all said and done, there is often too much said and too little done. The person who knows what to do for others is valuable, but the person who does it is priceless.

46

*"I like the dreams of the future
better than the history of the past."*

—THOMAS JEFFERSON

THOMAS JEFFERSON, a devout supporter of democracy, was the nation's 3rd president of the United States. At 33, he was an American founding father and principal author of the Declaration of Independence in 1776. The document outlines three fundamental rights of all Americans: "life, liberty, and the pursuit of happiness." Before serving as the president of the United States from 1801 to 1809, he was John Adam's second vice president and the first United States secretary of state under George Washington.

Born on April 13, 1743, at the Shadwell plantation in Goochland County, Virginia, Thomas Jefferson was a statesman, diplomat, lawyer, architect, and archaeologist. He grew to be 6'2" tall with a freckled face, sandy-colored hair, and a dignified demeanor. Thomas Jefferson was a wine lover and connoisseur of French food. In 1784, as Minister of France for the newly established United States of America, he lived in France for five years—two years after his wife of ten years, Martha Wayles Skelton, died—along with his 11-year-old daughter, Martha, known as Patsy. Upon returning to America before the French Revolution began in May 1789, French cuisine was featured within his home and later at his presidential dinner parties.

Many say that Thomas Jefferson inspired the new world with European-American classic dishes, such as vanilla ice cream, steak and fries, and macaroni and cheese. He also brought his passion for French wine to America and became known as one of the great wine experts. At his 5,000-acre plantation in Monticello, Virginia, Thomas Jefferson kept two vineyards.

Thomas Jefferson spoke, read, and wrote French, Greek, self-taught Italian, and German languages with a lifelong interest in linguistics. He was familiar with several American Indian vocabularies of his time. He was a quiet man and preferred to remain silent whenever possible. His correspondence and writings were eloquent, and he favored lending his pen rather than his voice to the patriot causes.

His first annual "State of the Union" address was set for December 1, 1801. Thomas Jefferson wrote his speech on parchment and, instead of delivering it himself before the 7th United States Congress in Washington, DC, he requested a clerk read it on his behalf. Cautiously, he did not want to give the impression that he was a king. So, in keeping to the Constitution which states that the president of the United States "shall from time to time give to the Congress information of the state of the union, and recommend to their consideration such measures as he shall judge necessary and expedient," he allowed members of Congress to contemplate his words and act accordingly.

As he explained, the State of the Union address and all subsequent correspondence between the legislative and executive branches would be through messengers. He cited that it was more convenient for all. In his words, he begged understanding to his decision, saying, "I have principal regard to the convenience of the legislature, to the economy of their time, to their relief from the embarrassment of immediate answers on subjects not yet fully before them, and to the benefits hence resulting to the public affairs, trusting that a procedure founded in these motives, will meet their approbation [approval]." Thomas Jefferson provided accompanying documents for consideration. The tradition of a representative delivering the president's speech continued for more than 100 years until the 28th president, Woodrow Wilson, delivered his State of the Union address in person.

Thomas Jefferson was not known to be a public speaker, but he was an avid reader and treasured books. During his lifetime, he assembled three libraries and had the most extensive personal collection of books in the United States in his time.

As a youth, much of his library consisted of works he inherited from his father and those bequeathed to him by George Wythe, a Virginia judge, noted classics scholar, and the first American law professor. His library totaled 200 volumes. His collection was destroyed when his Shadwell home burned in 1770. Within three years, he replenished his library with 1,250 titles, and by 1814, it had evolved into nearly 6,500 volumes. He organized his collection into three broad categories that corresponded with elements of the human mind—memory, reason, and imagination.

When the British invaded the Library of Congress during the "Burning of Washington" in 1814, Thomas Jefferson helped rebuild it by selling nearly all of the 6,500 books from his library collection to replace those lost. He immediately sought to rebuild his library with his favorites. Speaking of his library, he wrote to his closest friend, John Adams, "I cannot live without books." At his death, his new library had grown to nearly 2,000 books.

On July 4, 1826, the 50th anniversary of the Declaration of Independence, Thomas Jefferson died. He was 83. Several hours later that day, so, too, did John Adams die.

At various times in Thomas Jefferson's life, he documented his achievements, and on the threshold of his death, he designed his gravestone monument and epitaph. Inscribed were three achievements he considered to be his finest. It reads, "Here was buried Thomas Jefferson Author of the Declaration of American Independence of the Statute of Virginia for Religious Freedom and Father of the University of Virginia." Among his accomplishments, he did not mention his presidency of the United States.

As a relatively young man, Thomas Jefferson was thrust into a critical point in world history. He served a number of roles in the early United States government, including becoming president. But he will forever be remembered as the author of the Declaration of Independence. The genius of that document and his insight remains evident more than 250 years after he penned those immortal words. His quote mirrors his actions when, in the midst of war, strife, and dissension, he imagined and dreamed of better days ahead.

Too often, we assume that realists are people who see the worst of everything in the current day; and too often we assume dreamers hold an unrealistic fantasy of the future. Thomas Jefferson reminds us all in word and deed that success becomes possible when we fully understand the reality of the present moment while embracing the potential and promise of the future.

47

*"Intelligence without ambition
is a bird without wings."*

—SALVADOR DALI

SALVADOR DOMINGO FELIPE JACINTO DALÍ I DOMÈNECH, known simply as Salvador Dali, was a famous Spanish artist renowned for his technical skill, precise draftsmanship, and extraordinarily bizarre images, paintings, and lithographs. His iconic style of Surrealism was designed to capture, understand, and express his dreams, imagination, and subconscious. Always desiring attention, his flamboyancy and outrageous appearance guaranteed him the recognition and attention he craved.

He carried himself with poise and distinction in public, with arrogance beaming in his expression. He wore a long cape, used a walking stick, and sported jet black hair and a thin handlebar mustache stiffened and shaped with thick wax that enabled it to turn up toward his eyes. His mustache became as legendary as his paintings, and he remains one of the most famous artists of the 20th century. Unquestionably, he was the most eccentric and outrageous artist of all time. Perhaps his most extraordinary work of art was himself.

Though Salvador Dali produced significant paintings, his artistic range included graphic arts, film, sculptures, set designs, and photography. He wrote fiction, poetry, essays, and criticisms. In 1942, he wrote his autobiography titled, *The Secret Life of*

Salvador Dali. It was rumored that it was fictionalized, and the eccentric artist confused true and false memories.

Born May 11, 1904, in Figueres, Catalonia, Spain, he was the second son to his parents. His older brother, also named Salvador Dali, died at age 3, nine months before the artist was born. Having the same name as his deceased brother haunted the young boy throughout his life. Images of his brother appeared later in his works, including *Portrait of My Dead Brother*, completed in 1963. The grown-up image closely resembled the artist. A photo of his brother hung above his parents' bed, and the family often tearfully spoke of their firstborn. At times, Salvador Dali was uncertain of which son they were referencing.

When he was 5, he was further confused when his parents took him to visit his brother's grave. There, he saw his name inscribed on the gravestone, and his parents told him they believed he was the reincarnation of the first Salvador Dali, which explained why he received the same name.

Salvador Dali began painting at age 3. At 10, he was an accomplished painter, and his father arranged an art exhibition to display his work. Recognizing his brilliance, his mother sent him to art school. Later, he received his formal education in fine arts in Madrid. Salvador Dali refused his final exams, arguing that no teacher knew as much as he did. The school expelled him.

His primary influences were impressionism and the masters of the Renaissance. His interest led him to experiment with Cubism and Surrealism. His most notable work was the Surrealist painting, *The Persistence of Memory*, completed in 1931. The painting's central theme of melting clocks and ants was intended to express many representations. The ants symbolize decay, a common theme of many of his paintings, and the melting clocks convey the passing of time as one might experience it in a dream. Some theorize that timepieces in his works reference Einstein's theory of relatively—contemplating relationship between time and space.

In 1973, while in America, rock and roll gained his attention, and he summoned singer, songwriter, and actor Vincent Furnier, also known as Alice Cooper, to visit him. In his words, "I was nervous. I had met the Beatles and Elvis [Presley], but this was Salvador Dali. This was like my history. We were immediately his favorite band because we not only were loud and obnoxious and in your face, but we were really creepy."

Alice Cooper had created a persona beyond belief using freakish makeup and live snakes. "Our stage show was very surrealistic. I think it kind of reminded him of his paintings," Alice Cooper said. "He walked into the room, and he was wearing giraffe skin pants, Aladdin shoes that curled up, and a pair of purple socks that Elvis gave him. He announced, 'The Dali is here.'"

During the conversation, Alice Cooper went on to say, "he speaks one word in French, one word in Portuguese, one word in English, one word in Spanish. So, you're only picking up every fifth word. You have no idea what he's talking about." As Salvador Dali later explained, "Confusion is the greatest form of communication." And with this façade, it gave him the license to do anything, no matter how bizarre.

In 1936, Dali attended a premiere screening of Joseph Cornell's film, *Rose Hobart*. Salvador Dali knocked over the projector in a rage, saying, "My idea for a film is exactly that. I never wrote it down or told anyone, but it is as if he had stolen it!" He was known to become enraged rather unexpectedly, destroying along the way.

During a book promotion in Manhattan, New York, for Robert Descharnes' 1962 book *The World of Salvador Dali*, he demonstrated his odd behavior by appearing on a bed hooked up to a machine that monitored and recorded his brain waves and blood pressure. As he autographed the book for customers, he gave them the ticker tape chart reading.

Frequently, Salvador Dali avoided paying the check at a restaurant. Instead, he made drawings on the bill and left the restaurant without paying. His theory was that the establishment would find his work of art so valuable that they would forgive the amount owed, which they did. His declaration of his genius was a vital characteristic of his personality. He would boast, "Every morning upon awakening, I experience a supreme pleasure: that of being Salvador Dali."

Salvador Dali's iconic image rekindled a global cultural phenomenon from the 2020 fictional Spanish television crime drama series, "Money Heist." In it, a lovable group of thieves and their mild-mannered professor disguised themselves with masks resembling the Spanish artist Salvador Dali, featuring his wide eyes and famously exaggerated turned-up handlebar mustache. Each code-named for cities Tokyo, Berlin, Nairobi, Rio, Denver, Helsinki, and Oslo, the eight robbers held up the Royal Mint of Spain and the Bank of Spain. Salvador Dali's likeness was chosen because he was highly recognized worldwide, and it symbolized a cultural reference to Spain. At each film location, fans of both the movie and Salvador Dali lined the streets with identical masks. More than thirty years after his death, Salvador Dali lives on in his work and unique image.

Throughout his career, Salvador Dali created 1,500 paintings. His last known painting was completed in May 1983, although some critics are skeptical of its origin since he was presumed to have suffered from severe tremors at the time.

In 1984, Salvador Dali fell into a deep depression after the death of his estranged wife, Gala, and retreated to the Púbol Castle she had purchased long before her death in 1982. Gala had been the only person ever to see the shy and vulnerable side of Salvador Dali's personality. Through her care and business savvy, she had transformed her husband from a Spanish artist into a multimillionaire.

In August of that year, a fire broke out at Púbol Castle. Salvador Dali suffered severe burns on 20 percent of his body. Upon release from the hospital, he was moved to a room in the Torre Galatea, annexing his Dali Theatre-Museum in Figueres, Spain. Five years later, on January 23, 1989, Salvador Dali died of heart failure. He was 84. According to a documentary on his life, "Salvador Dali would be buried as he lived, on center stage. He asked to be interred in his museum, beneath his art, under the feet of his admiring fans." American Salvador Dali fans can view his masterpieces at the Salvador Dali Museum in St. Petersburg, Florida.

——— A ———

The true measure of any artist is the impact their work has upon those who experience it. As a blind person myself, I regret that I have never had the ability and privilege of personally experiencing Salvador Dali's work. However, I have been present in museums around the world when I experience the impact of his work as family, friends, and other museum patrons looked upon his masterpieces. Few artists' works have ever initiated more thought, discussion, and inspired interpretation than that of Salvador Dali.

His quote, *"Intelligence without ambition is a bird without wings,"* reminds us that being inspired is a gift we have been given, and taking action on that inspiration is a gift we are giving the world. Salvador Dali brought his inspiration to life on canvas and left it behind for us all to enjoy, cherish, and derive our own inspiration.

48

*"I have noticed even people who claim
everything is predestined, and that we can do
nothing to change it, look before they cross the road."*

—STEPHEN HAWKING

STEPHEN WILLIAM HAWKING was born on January 8, 1942, in Oxford, England, on the 300th anniversary of the death of the "father of modern physics," Galileo Galilei. It was a noted perception he was proud to relate to others. He grew to become a British scientist, professor, author, and one of the most significant theoretical physicists. He pioneered theories in physics and cosmology, devoting more than fifty years of his life to science. He wrote or coauthored fifteen science-related books, making his ideas and findings accessible worldwide.

Many of his theories revolutionized the way the universe is viewed, and he stirred national attention with his black hole and relativity insights, for which he is best known. His quantum mechanics theorem, developed in 1971, concludes that the total area of all black holes in the universe cannot decrease. Instead, it increases in proportion to its surface area. Contradictory to Albert Einstein's "Theory of General Relativity" that theorized the surface area of a black hole can shrink over time.

Throughout his career, Stephen Hawking held prestigious academic posts, was appointed Commander of the Order of the British Empire, a distinction awarded to individuals having a prominent role at a national level, and earned the U.S. Presidential Medal of Freedom in 2009. All the while, his body was failing as he suffered from the debilitating motor neuron disease known as Amyotrophic Lateral Sclerosis (ALS). Despite his failing health, he received a "first-class" bachelor of arts degree in physics, which opened the door to his graduate work at Trinity Hall in Cambridge. He obtained a Ph.D. in applied mathematics and theoretical physics and specialized in general relativity and cosmology. Believing at the time that he would not live to complete his doctorate, he declined its pursuit.

Until his death in 2018, he served as Director of Research at the Centre for Theoretical Cosmology, University of Cambridge.

The eldest of four children, he was born into a family of intellectuals. His parents graduated from Oxford University, and his father became a respected medical researcher specializing in tropical diseases. The Hawking family, as one close family friend recalled, "Were an 'eccentric' bunch. Dinner was often eaten in silence, each of the Hawkings intently reading a book. The family car was an old London taxi, and their home in St. Albans was a three-story fixer-upper that never quite got fixed. The Hawkings also housed bees in the basement and produced fireworks in the greenhouse."

By his own account, Stephen Hawking revealed that he did not learn to read until he was 8 years old, and at St. Albans elementary school, he was an average student studying only an hour per day. Nonetheless, he was given the nickname "Einstein" by his classmates because he demonstrated an overwhelming aptitude for grasping issues of space and time.

In his final examination at the University College in Oxford, his score was such that he finally passed an oral exam after taking the test twice. In the end, Stephen Hawking realized the importance of applying himself academically, and at 17, he aced his Oxford entrance exam and received a scholarship to study physics.

In 1963, while in his early 20s, Stephen Hawking became increasingly clumsy, falling frequently. When his father noticed it, he took him for tests. Eventually, doctors discovered the cause, and he was diagnosed with ALS and told that the nerves controlling his muscles would slowly shut down. His prognosis was not good, and he was presumed to have little more than two years to live. He felt he had been dealt an unjust hand in life. Inevitably, the disease began to affect the movements of his hands, feet, and limbs. As it advanced, the condition destroyed his nerve cells, and his muscles grew weaker. Though it affected his chewing, swallowing, breathing, and speaking over time, he continued to have a keen mind.

While at a New Year's party in 1962, Stephen Hawking met Jane Wilde, his St. Alban friend's younger sister. Fully aware of his prognosis and despite the challenges that lay ahead, knowing that she would carry the responsibilities of home and family on her shoulders, Jane Wilde accepted Stephen Hawking's marriage proposal in October 1964. His relationship rejuvenated his will to achieve as much as possible in the short time doctors had expected him to live, saying it gave him "something to live for."

At their wedding, held on July 14, 1965, Stephen Hawking already felt the effects of his disease and walked with a cane. In sharing his thoughts about his illness, he claimed that it gave him focus. He once said, "Before my condition was diagnosed, I had been very bored with life. There had not seemed to be anything worth doing." The couple was married for thirty years and shared three children.

Stephen Hawking was concerned that ALS would diminish his genius; however, it is unknown whether he took the Intelligence Quotient (IQ) test to determine whether his intellect was affected by the disease. Though not an exact science, approximately seven tests gauge one's ability to use information and logic to answer questions or make predictions. Scores over 140 indicate intellectual genius. According to the Stanford-Binet Intelligence Scale, scores of 90 to 109 are considered "normal or average." Stephen Hawking discounted IQ scores. When asked his IQ in a 2004 interview for the *New York Times*, he remarked, "People who boast about their IQ are losers." Nonetheless, it has been reported that Professor Stephen Hawking and Albert Einstein shared identical IQ scores of 160.

Despite his disabilities—being confined to an electric wheelchair and requiring a computerized speech synthesizer to speak—Stephen Hawking maintained a sense of humor. In December 2006, while visiting Jerusalem, he spoke of his physical limitations. Amusingly, he shared his thoughts on the pros and cons of being disabled. He said, "The only advantage of my disability is that I do not get put on a lot of boring committees," and of the cons, "I cannot go anywhere in the world without being recognized. It is not enough for me to wear dark glasses and a wig. The wheelchair gives me away."

In June 2014, Stephen Hawking appeared on *Last Week Tonight with John Oliver*. On the interview series titled "People Who Think Good," John Oliver asked, "You've stated that you believe there could be an infinite number of parallel universes. Does this mean that there is a universe out there where I am smarter than you?" Stephen Hawking replied, "Yes, and also a universe where you're funny."

Stephen Hawking, incredibly, survived an incurable motor neuron condition for fifty-five years. He died on March 14, 2018, at age 76. Services were held at Westminster Abbey, and his ashes were interred in the Abbey's nave between the graves of Sir Isaac Newton and Charles Darwin. Inscribed on his stone marker are the words "Here lies what was mortal of Stephen Hawking 1942-2018," In his death directive, he requested that the "Bekenstein-Hawking Entropy Equation" be his epitaph and etched on the stone. In June 2018, Stephen Hawking's words were set to music by Greek composer Vangelis and beamed into space from a European space agency satellite dish in Spain to reach the nearest black hole, 1A 0620-00—a binary star system in the constellation of Monoceros.

Stephen Hawking often said, "When you are faced with the possibility of an early death, it makes you realize that life is worth living and that there are a lot of things you want to do." Stephen Hawking succeeded and lived life to the fullest.

—— A ——

I've had the privilege over the last few years to become affiliated with a university where, on a regular basis, I work with esteemed professors and students from around the world. It takes a very learned person and accomplished thinker to even begin to understand the genius of Stephen Hawking. In the midst of his own physical disabilities in which his body failed to respond as he wanted it to, he found a way to release his mind and thought power in ways that impacted the world and will continue to change the way we understand the nature of the universe for generations to come.

His quote, *"I have noticed even people who claim everything is predestined, and that we can do nothing to change it, look before they cross the road,"* encourages us all to challenge the things we think, know, and believe. In our contentious world today, we tend to criticize people who change their opinions. In reality, someone whose thoughts, ideas, or opinions never change has ceased to learn, develop, and grow.

49

"Aerodynamically, the bumblebee shouldn't be able to fly, but the bumblebee doesn't know it, so it goes on flying anyway."

—MARY KAY ASH

MARY KAY ASH was an entrepreneur and business leader who built a multinational cosmetic company, initially called "Beauty by Mary Kay" and later renamed Mary Kay Inc., befittingly referred to as simply "Mary Kay." With little capital and a skincare formula, she created an opportunity for every willing woman to build a profitable business using Mary Kay's Golden Rule philosophy based on kindness and sharing with others. The company's training programs and marketing materials allow each woman to write her own success story.

Her transformational multilevel marketing business model continues to empower women. It allows them to purchase cosmetics at wholesale prices, sell at retail value, set flexible work schedules around their personal and family lives, and achieve financial success by giving their customers the service and attention they deserve. In the words of Mary Kay, "I wanted to provide an open-ended opportunity to women, to help them achieve anything they were smart enough to do. I didn't think it was fair for women to earn less than a man doing the same work. And I was tired of people telling me that I thought like a woman."

The youngest of four children, she was born Mary Kathlyn Wagner on May 12, 1918, in Hot Wells, Texas. Within two years, her family moved to Houston. When she was 3 years old, her father, Edward, contracted tuberculosis and was sent to a tuberculosis sanatorium for four years, leaving her mother, Lula, to support the family. Lula took a job as a restaurant manager, working fourteen hours a day. As a female worker, she was not adequately compensated for her contribution. Seeing her mother's struggles, along with her own experiences working the same jobs as men but receiving less pay, gave her the incentive to make a better life for herself and countless women worldwide.

At 17, Mary Kathlyn Wagner married promising radio personality Ben Rogers, and they had three children. During World War II, he was called to service. While her husband served in the United States Army, she began her career selling child psychology books door to door to earn commissions to support her family. Upon his return from the war, the marriage ended. It became the lowest point in Mary Kay's life.

Fortunately, direct sales gave her the flexibility to earn money and spend time with her children. After changing jobs several times—first selling books, then cookware, to cleaning products—Mary Kay found success at Stanley Home Products. The job required her to lug heavy household products into private homes to host demonstrations. The work was challenging, and she, ultimately, enjoyed an excellent reputation as one of their top sales performers.

Each year, Stanley Home Products held a seminar. To attend, Mary Kay borrowed the money. It was well worth the cost, for the event set the tone for her future and the future of Mary Kay Cosmetics. As founder of Stanley Home Products, Frank Stanley Beveridge, spoke, his message for Mary Kay was twofold. The first lesson was that "To be successful, hitch your wagon to a star." During the seminar, the "Queen of Sales" was announced. As the top performer of the company, the woman won an alligator bag. Mary Kay wished that bag was hers. After thinking about the message, she hitched her wagon to the "Queen of Sales" as her mentor. She wanted to know everything that made the woman successful, and the woman was happy to share.

She learned something else from Frank Stanley Beveridge. When she let him know that the following year she would be the woman crowned top salesperson, his response was, "You know. Somehow, I think you will." That, along with her mother's words to her that, "You can do it," was the encouragement she needed. The following year, Mary Kay was crowned "Queen of Sales." She learned that day that sharing with others was the critical element to success—share your talents, dreams, secrets, and be accountable to your goals.

Mary Kay shared the story of one day when she stood in a long line of people for three hours to give a congratulatory handshake to a newly named vice president of Stanley Home Products. As she approached him, she extended her hand, and he, too, in turn, but he looked past her focusing his attention on how many more people were in line. He never noticed whose hand he was shaking. After being inspired to wait for those three hours, he ignored her.

She learned another valuable lesson on that day, and she vowed that if she ever became someone who people wanted to shake her hand, she would focus her attention on them and make them feel important. She taught all Mary Kay Independent Beauty Consultants to "Pretend that every single person has a sign around his or her neck that says, 'Make me feel important.' Not only will you succeed in sales, you will succeed in life."

In 1952, based on her reputation of success with Stanley Home Products, Mary Kay was offered a position with the

World Gifts Company selling home decorating accessories. She spent more than a decade in sales but resigned in protest when a man she had trained received a promotion above her, earning twice her salary. She had been overlooked simply because she was a woman. As a result of that experience, in 1963, then age 45, Mary Kay decided to retire to write a book relating her experiences in direct sales. She wanted to help women succeed in business and to let women know that "Success was not a masculine privilege."

After listing the pros and cons of the companies she had worked for, she devised solutions to resolve the cons. Instead of writing the book, what she had created was a business plan—a vision that would enrich her life and the lives of countless women. It included equal pay for equal work, something America was not offering its female workforce. That same year, Mary Kay married for the second time to chemist George Hallenbeck, which lasted only two months. Tragically, one month before launching her business, her husband died of a heart attack. He was to be her administrative person of the newly developed company.

Mary Kay used her $5,000 savings to purchase product jars, literature, and sales manuals and recruit nine women to sell products. She bought a skincare formula developed by an Arkansas hide tanner named J. W. Heath for $500. She selected the color soft pink for her product packaging, saying, "The containers would be so attractive that women would want to display them in their bathrooms." She then set out to open a storefront cosmetic company in Dallas, Texas. She called it "Beauty by Mary Kay." Mary Kay found that she needed more capital to continue her venture, but this was a time in history when women were not permitted to sign their names to bank loans. Mary Kay's son, Ben, said, "I think you can do anything," and offered $4,500 to complete her dream.

All of her children had faith in their mother. On September 13, 1965, one month following the death of her husband, the "Beauty by Mary Kay" doors opened. Ben became the warehouse manager, her son, Richard, quit his job with a reputable insurance company to run the administrative side of the business and fulfill orders in the absence of George Hallenbeck. Her daughter, Marilyn, began selling Mary Kay's cosmetics. With their help, her new line of skincare products, nine Independent Beauty Consultants, the doctrine putting faith first, family second, and career third, Mary Kay turned the color pink into gold.

She implemented her vision for success. Her priority was to train each Independent Beauty Consultant and approach selling with a commitment to serve the needs of their customers. Sales totaled $198,000 in the first year. In 1969, the company's success led Mary Kay to the Cadillac dealership. When she asked the salesman to have her new Cadillac Coupe Deville car painted in soft pink, he touted all of the reasons why that was not a good idea. She insisted, nonetheless, and after her team saw the car, they, too, wanted a pink Cadillac. As the company grew more successful, the Mary Kay Career Car Program proved that "pink is the color of success." Subsequently, in the United States, Mary Kay continues to give pink Cadillacs to top achievers, pink Toyotas in Taiwan, pink Fords in Argentina, pink Volvos in the Nordic countries, and pink Mercedes in Germany.

Mary Kay married for the third time in 1966 to Melville Jerome Ash. One day she was in an airport gift shop early in the company's history and saw a plaque with a bumblebee pictured. The caption read, "Aerodynamically, the bumblebee shouldn't be able to fly, but the bumblebee doesn't know it, so it goes on flying anyway." As she told the story, she thought it was "A marvelous symbol of women who go right on flying even though all scientific evidence would say it's not possible. As a result of this, my husband, Mel, bought me a beautiful diamond bumblebee [pin] one year. It was a huge bee, and I said, 'Oh Honey, you've made a mistake here. Everybody is going to want one of these bees.' He replied, 'No, there's just one Queen to the hive.'" From that, Mary Kay began awarding all of the women who rose to be top performers a large diamond bumblebee at the company's annual seminar.

Mary Kay changed the world of business by creating opportunities for women. When asked how she succeeded so quickly, she said, "The answer is I was middle-aged, had varicose veins, and I didn't have time to fool around. Have you heard the definition of a woman's needs? From birth to fourteen, she needs good parents and good health, from fourteen to forty, she needs good looks, from forty to sixty, she needs personality, and I'm here to tell you that after sixty, she needs cash."

As one Senior National Sales Director of Mary Kay Cosmetic described achieving financial success, "Service the other person's needs, and you'll never have to worry about the money you make. Money is the pleasure that you send into the lives of others."

Mary Kay stepped down as CEO of Mary Kay, Inc. in 1987. She continued to be an active part of the business until she suffered a stroke in 1996. That same year, she established the Mary Kay Charitable Foundation, supporting women's cancer research and efforts to end domestic violence.

On November 22, 2001, at 83, Mary Kay Ash died, but her legacy lives on. She will forever be remembered for her vision. She created new opportunities, blazed the trail of success for women everywhere, and led the way for economic freedom for women worldwide.

What has made Mary Kay Cosmetics so successful is un-matched opportunities for women, top-quality products, a continual teaching approach for Independent Beauty Consultants at all levels of the organization, and a fundamental set of core values. Her business concept and history are studied in universities all across the country.

— A —

Over the last twenty-five years, I have spoken at countless arena events and corporate conventions. They all seem to run together in my mind, with a few memorable exceptions. I will never forget speaking at a Mary Kay convention in Dallas in an arena with more than 10,000 highly successful and motivated women. At that time, the company founded by Mary Kay Ash had been responsible for more women around the world reaching financial independence than any other organization.

I was struck by the overwhelming sense of optimism and expectation projected by the thousands of Mary Kay associates. Like the bumblebee mentioned in the quote, they believed that all of their goals were possible and attainable, so, therefore, they were. Mary Kay Ash was truly a trailblazer who created a unique organization the likes of which had never existed before. Her belief in her mission overcame any logical or practical thoughts that might have held her back. She thought she could, so she did—and today there are hundreds of thousands of Mary Kay associates who are a living legacy to the foresight and vision of Mary Kay Ash.

50

NELSON MANDELA was born Rolihlahla Mandela. His first name in the Bantu language, Xhosa, means "pulling the branch of a tree" or, more commonly translated, "troublemaker." The name "Nelson" was given to him by his teacher, Miss Mdingane when he attended primary school in the tiny village of Qunu. The British educational system customary give all school-aged children Christian names, and he became known as Nelson Mandela.

Born into the Thembu royal family in the small village of Mvezo, Union of South Africa, on July 18, 1918, Nelson Mandela grew to become a social rights activist, political leader, philanthropist, and the first black president of South Africa elected in a fully representative democratic election.

He was born to royalty, but his father, the counselor to tribal chiefs, lost his title and fortune over a colonial magistrate conflict. The family was forced to move to the tiny village of Qunu, where they lived in a hut among grazing livestock, drank from the springs and streams on the land, and cooked locally harvested foods outdoors.

At age 12, his father died of lung disease, and Chief Jongintaba Dalindyebo adopted Nelson Mandela as a favor to his father for recommending him to the position. The young boy quickly adapted to the sophisticated environment in the provincial capital of Thembuland, and it was there that he grew interested in African history.

The father who had adopted him was grooming his son to inherit power. He had methodically mapped Nelson Mandela's life, a duty within his right as tribal custom permitted. As a member of the Thembu royalty, he attended the Wesleyan mission school achieving academic success through "plain hard work," as he recalled. In 1939, he enrolled at the University of Fort Hare, a university educationally comparable to Harvard University. He focused on Roman-Dutch law, hoping to land a job as an interpreter or clerk. To his dismay, he returned from the university to find that Jongintaba had arranged for his marriage. He was further outraged by the confining goals set for him. Feeling trapped, he fled the royal court to study law in Johannesburg, enrolling at the University of the Witwatersrand.

In 1952, he formed the first black law firm of Mandela and Tambo, partnering with Oliver Tambo, whom he met while attending the University of Fort Hare. Their firm provided free and low-cost legal counsel to unrepresented black people.

Nelson Mandela joined the African National Congress, a political group that peaceably opposed the government's policy of racial segregation known as apartheid, the then rigid policy of segregation. It economically and politically oppressed the non-white population of his country. Feeling that the movement was not moving quickly enough, Mandela urged the African National Congress to form a military unit to challenge the all-white government.

After returning from military training in Algeria in 1961, Nelson Mandela orchestrated a national worker's strike that lasted three days. For this act, he was arrested and sentenced to five years in prison. In 1963, Nelson Mandela and ten other

African National Congress leaders were arrested. Again, Nelson Mandela was tried and convicted, this time for sabotage and plotting to overthrow the government. He was sentenced to life in prison.

Nelson Mandela spent the first eighteen years in jail at the brutal Robben Island prison. He was contained in a small cell without a bed or plumbing. He was forced to do hard labor in a quarry and was permitted a visitor for thirty minutes one time each year. He could write letters to his family every six months, but prison officials highly scrutinized the letters. Over time, the prison allowed him to write to friends and associates, but words of a political nature were forbidden.

Nelson Mandela successfully smuggled statements and letters to the outside world with assistance from other prisoners and visitors and continued his fight. In 1976, however, his 500-page autobiography manuscript, miniaturized to 50 pages, was sent with a departing prisoner. The original manuscript was soon discovered by the warden buried in a garden. As a result of the infraction, Nelson Mandela and several others lost their study rights for four years, suspending his correspondence law program studies from the University of London. This punishment did not break his spirit, but it led him to protest the living conditions of Robben Island. In 1982, he was sent to Pollsmoor Prison for six years, and in 1988 he was moved to a cottage, where he lived under house arrest.

By 1989, F.W. de Klerk was president of South Africa, and he dismantled apartheid. He lifted the ban on African National Congress and suspended executions. On February 11, 1990, Nelson Mandela was released as a political prisoner after serving twenty-seven years of incarceration. From behind bars, Nelson Mandela had continued to influence political events and people in the fight for full citizenship, redistribution of land, trade union rights, and free and mandatory education for all children. Eventually, the government abandoned its racial barriers.

In 1991, the year following his release from prison, Nelson Mandela was elected president of the African National Congress. His long-time friend and colleague, Oliver Tambo, served as national chairperson by his side.

In 1993, Nelson Mandela and President de Klerk jointly received the Nobel Peace Prize for their part in dismantling apartheid in South Africa. Nelson Mandela demonstrated his heroism by risking his life for equality, liberty, and justice for his people.

Nelson Mandela received the nation's highest honor when he was elected president of the South African people from 1994 to 1999. As published in Biography.com, history remembers him as "The man who refused to inherit princely powers with his tribe, was elected President of his entire nation chosen by voters who proudly marked on their ballets the name Nelson Mandela."

At age 79, he declined a second presidential term. Instead, he became an elder statesman and focused his efforts on combating poverty and HIV/AIDS through the Nelson Mandela Foundation.

Deeply respected within South Africa, Nelson Mandela has been described as the "Father of the Nation." He paid a substantial price for his role in fighting for civil rights, equality, and justice, and it had taken a toll on his health. He had contracted tuberculosis while imprisoned, receiving the lowest level of healthcare from prison employees.

On December 5, 2013, Nelson Mandela, suffering from a prolonged respiratory infection, died at age 95. He will forever be an inspiration for his commitment to his undying beliefs and actions. On the day of Mandela's death, South African President

Jacob Zuma released a statement speaking to Nelson Mandela's legacy: "Wherever we are in the country, wherever we are in the world, let us reaffirm his vision of a society…in which none is exploited, oppressed, or dispossessed by another."

———— A ————

In this first volume filled with powerful quotes that have endured throughout the centuries, it was a challenge to find someone appropriate and worthy of having the last word. If anyone throughout history could have been justified for feeling hatred, resentment, and bitterness, it would be Nelson Mandela. His optimism, sense of justice, and hope of a better day kept him alive and prepared him to become a world leader and an iconic historical figure.

Mandela's ability to respond with love throughout the horrific ordeal he endured allowed him to not only experience his own freedom but to be the catalyst to free his nation from tyranny and racism. If we can believe in Mandela's words and follow his example, we can hold on to hope until the reality around us matches the dreams inside of us.

CONCLUSION

AS YOU CAN SEE, quotes that have shaped our world come from all occupations, lifestyles, and generations. As Jim Stovall might say, *"As you go through your day, consider how your words and actions may influence people for many generations."*

ABOUT THE AUTHORS

JIM STOVALL

In spite of blindness, Jim Stovall has been a National Olympic weightlifting champion, a successful investment broker, the president of the Emmy Award-winning Narrative Television Network, and a highly sought-after author and platform speaker. He is the author of 50 books including the bestseller *The Ultimate Gift*, which is now a major motion picture from 20th Century Fox starring James Garner and Abigail Breslin. Five of his other novels have also been made into movies with two more in production.

Steve Forbes, president and CEO of *Forbes* magazine, says, "Jim Stovall is one of the most extraordinary men of our era." For his work in making television accessible to our nation's 13 million blind and visually impaired people, the President's Committee on Equal Opportunity selected Jim Stovall as the Entrepreneur of the Year. Jim Stovall has been featured in *The Wall Street Journal*, *Forbes* magazine, *USA Today*, and has been seen on *Good Morning America*, CNN, and *CBS Evening News*. He was also chosen as the International Humanitarian of the Year, joining Jimmy Carter, Nancy Reagan, and Mother Teresa as recipients of this honor.

Jim Stovall can be reached at 918-627-1000 or Jim@JimStovall.com.

KATHY JOHNSON

Kathy Johnson has been a prominent business writer for a number of years. She found great success in corporate America with positions of managerial responsibility and charge at various financial institutions developing and directing marketing programs, always maintaining a consistent focus on writing and scripting.

Diversely, Kathy Johnson founded and developed several business-to-business magazines, including the deep-rooted regional magazine, *BusinessWise*, in Indiana, serving as owner and editor. She has edited books, magazines, and articles for various authors, including Jim Stovall.

Kathy Johnson earned her Core Competency certification and became a Dale Carnegie instructor in its leadership management, relationship strengthening, and sales training courses.

After completion of her academic novella, *Seasons to Remember*, Kathy earned her bachelor of science degree from the University of Evansville, Evansville, Indiana, and her master's degree in organizational management from Oakland City University in Oakland City, Indiana.

Leaving corporate America, Kathy Johnson pursued her long-time passion for drama, suspense, and romance in her historical novel, *Destination Alcatraz*.

Kathy Johnson currently lives in Minnesota, and she can be reached at KathyJohnson@kjjohnson.net.

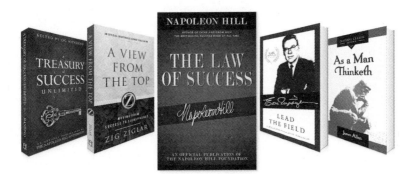